WAR IN THE PACIFIC

The most important, explosive, and strategic battles of World War Two took place in the Pacific arena, as the seemingly invincible Japanese sought to expand their notorious empire. Now this astonishing era comes to life in a breathtakingly authentic new series by noted historian Edwin P. Hoyt that places the reader in the heart of the earth-shattering conflict—a dramatic, detailed chronicle of military brilliance and extraordinary human courage on the bloody battlefields of land and sea.

VOLUME VIII

MacARTHUR'S RETURN

WAR IN THE PACIFIC

VOLUME VIII

MacARTHUR'S RETURN

EDWIN P. HOYT

AVON BOOKS ◆ NEW YORK

WAR IN THE PACIFIC, VOLUME 8: MacARTHUR'S RETURN is an original publication of Avon Books. This work has never before appeared in book form.

AVON BOOKS
A division of
The Hearst Corporation
1350 Avenue of the Americas
New York, New York 10019

First Avon Books Printing: July 1992

AVON TRADEMARK REG. U.S. PAT. OFF. AND IN OTHER COUNTRIES, MARCA REGISTRADA, HECHO EN U.S.A.

Printed in the U.S.A.

RA 10 9 8 7 6 5 4 3 2 1

CONTENTS

CHAPTER ONE

The Road to Australia

For more than a year General Douglas MacArthur, commander of the armed forces in the Philippines and former U.S. Army chief of staff, had been expecting a Japanese assault on the Philippines. Until the summer of 1941 MacArthur's official post was field marshal of the Philippine Army, but that July, President Franklin D. Roosevelt recalled MacArthur to active duty with the U.S. Army and placed him in command of all American and Philippine forces in the Far East as a warning to Japan.

The American army and navy defense plans had written off the Philippines as indefensible against the attack by the Japanese that was expected, and that was a cornerstone of American Far Eastern policy in 1941. MacArthur had been quarreling with that policy for years. The Philippines were defensible, he said, and since 1935 he had been building up the Philippines defense with local troops. To others, it seemed a wild and wooly dream. The Filipinos did not all speak the same language. Most of the soldiers could not read or write. The American support for the Philippines defense was anything but generous; there were shortages of everything. Yet MacArthur serenely depicted great progress in his military buildup over six years. And, as the Japanese threat became stronger in the summer of 1941, MacArthur began to get some support from within the army establishment. A large force of the new B-17 bombers that had been consigned to the islands began arriving. MacArthur predicted that by April 1942 the Philippines would be ready to resist a Japanese invasion.

The Japanese did not give him so much time: They attacked on December 8, a few hours after hitting Pearl Harbor. Almost immediately the Philippines air defenses were destroyed because there was no cogent air defense plan or reasonable radar and communications facilities. The messages from coast watchers and other observers were transmitted by the civilian telephone network, for example.

The American plan for the defense of the Philippines called for MacArthur to retreat to the Bataan Peninsula and hold out there. MacArthur wanted to hold out until help came from America. But the navy, in its Plan Orange for war against Japan, had presupposed the overrunning of the Philippines and a long fight back across the Central Pacific.

The army plan for defense on Bataan and the navy plan were the only definite planning that took place. The army sent a force of B-17s to the Philippines but there was no cogent plan for their use. Major General Lewis H. Brereton, the army air corps commander in the Far East, had the idea he would attack Formosa's airfields with his B-17s, but he had no maps or any intelligence about the Japanese dispositions. His dream was forlorn from the very beginning.

What happened was unusually dismal. When the Japanese first attacked, on December 8, the B-17s took to the air and scuttled for airfields to the south. But when the attack ended they came back and parked as they had before, neatly on the runways and aprons, in lines. In the second big air raid they were caught at Clark Field and half of all the B-17s in the islands were destroyed on the ground.

The fighter planes fared scarcely better. They too were lined up because of the military preoccupation with sabotage that afflicted both Hawaii and the Philippines, and thus proved easy prey for the second big Japanese air raid against Clark Field.

From the beginning the Japanese had air superiority, and would have had it even had the blunders not been made. The

Japanese naval air force devoted to the Philippines was too powerful. As bravely as the American pilots fought, they were no match for the enemy, whose Zero fighters were superior to anything the Americans then had.

In December MacArthur moved to Bataan. The American position was very strong, and the Japanese were defeated time and again at Bataan until hunger and disease set in.

General MacArthur called on Washington to launch an immediate offensive against the Japanese, bomb their cities with carrier planes, and concentrate on the war in the Pacific. But he was unaware that President Roosevelt perceived the Nazi threat in Europe as the greater danger. Because of that threat and the growing desperation of Britain, Prime Minister Winston Churchill was able to win a great diplomatic victory by persuading Roosevelt that the Pacific theater must be left to whatever defenses existed, and that the joint effort must be made against Germany.

MacArthur kept up a barrage of demands on Washington, but it did not change any plans. The pattern was set; the Philippines had been written off by the Joint Chiefs of Staff. Only a handful of supplies came in, mostly by submarine, and there were no reinforcements of planes, ships, or men.

Early in December the Asiatic Fleet, except for the submarines, had been sent to Java to join the British and Dutch defense forces there and try to halt the Japanese juggernaut. Early in January Admiral Thomas C. Hart moved down, too, and the army was left in virtual isolation on Bataan fighting the Japanese. General MacArthur did not remain on Bataan past an initial inspection. He moved to the fortress of Corregidor, where he holed up in the tunnels there. His troops developed a great contempt for him and referred to him as "Dugout Doug," but not a word of this feeling got out to the United States.

In March 1942 President Roosevelt ordered MacArthur to abandon his troops fighting the hopeless battle of the Philippines and go to Australia to take charge of the American military efforts there. It was conceived that the road

back to the Philippines would begin from "down under."
MacArthur left, but in typical fashion he exceeded his
orders and took his entire personal staff with him, thus
depriving Lieutenant General Jonathan Wainwright of much
needed support. MacArthur obviously knew the fall of the
Philippines was near and was determined to keep around
him these men who were personally loyal only to him.

MacArthur went to Australia, and in April Bataan surrendered. In May General Wainwright surrendered Corregidor.
The Japanese had conquered more than they expected, and
in a shorter time than they had expected. For example,
Rabaul was not on their original list of targets, but so
fast did the victories come that spring that it was occupied
almost without opposition. Still, the American defense of
the Philippines was notable in that it was the only area in
which the Westerners had stood up to the Japanese and
tampered with the Japanese timetable. It did not make
any difference to Tokyo in the long run that the islands
took two months longer to occupy than planned. But it
was an embarrassment internationally, and it cost General
Masaharu Homma his command; the displeasure of the
Imperial General Headquarters was such that he was not
employed again during the war.

General MacArthur moved by PT boat and B-17 bomber
to Australia, where he announced that he had come away
from the Philippines by presidential order. "But I shall
return," he announced. It was one of those meaningless
statements, a promise for the future with no dates attached.
But such was the awe in which MacArthur was held in
Japan, as well as in America, that his statement had a
profound effect on the morale of the Americans and on
the planning of the Japanese Imperial Staff. At once the
taking of Papua, New Guinea, and a potential assault on
Australia became matters for planning to be sure that this
difficult enemy did not return.

CHAPTER TWO

New Guinea Operations

After General MacArthur reached New Guinea in the middle of March 1942 and held a press conference to announce, "I shall return," he also told associates and the world that he had been selected to head the American offensive against Japan.

This was not strictly accurate. In the first place there was no offensive against Japan in March; all that could be said was that the Pacific Fleet was conducting some carrier raids, and not very effective ones at that, and planning for the Doolittle raid on Tokyo, which also would not be very effective. The "Battling Bastards of Bataan" were still holding out and would for another month, and Corregidor would be held until May, thus creating the only embarrassment of the Japanese lightning campaign and causing the disgrace of General Homma, the Japanese commander, who was never afterward employed in the war.

MacArthur would not have command of the American offensive against Japan; quite to the contrary, his immediate role would be to defend Australia against the Japanese, whose offensive had been so remarkably successful in its first stages that the timetable was completely upset. It seemed so easy that they moved into the second stage of operations, which had not been planned to take place for months, and occupied Rabaul on New Britain Island in the center of the Bismarck Archipelago. Rabaul now became the major Japanese base in the Southern Pacific, and they planned to fan out from there to capture New Guinea, Fiji, Samoa, the French possessions in the South Pacific, and Australia if all went well. One of their first moves was to send troops to occupy Lae and Salamaua on the east coast of New Guinea, a move that was made before MacArthur arrived in Australia.

When MacArthur arrived he did not have much. The best Australian troops had been sent to the Middle East to fight the Italians and the Germans, and the Australian army training program was just under way. The Aussies did have the Seventh Division and this became MacArthur's principal striking force. He had also been sent two divisions from America, but the first of them, the Thirty-second Division, was ill-trained and not equipped for warfare in the jungle. When it was committed to action too soon, the immediate result was a series of stunning defeats by the highly trained and well-armed Japanese dug in on the east coast. By midsummer the Japanese had launched two attempts to take over Port Moresby, one by sea to Milne Bay, an invasion that was resisted by the Australians primarily and by the new U.S. Fifth Air Force under Lieutenant General George Kenney, and one over land along the Kokoda trail that runs along the ridges of the Papua mountain ranges. They had established extremely strong defensive points at Buna and Gona, with blockhouses constructed of concrete and palm logs, which would resist anything but a bomb or a direct tank assault, and the Allies were short of tanks and big field guns. The Japanese also had devised a defensive perimeter that consisted of outposts out in front of the blockhouses, many of them in the palms, armed with rifles and light machine guns. They would let the Allied soldiers approach, bypassing them, and then when the firing opened from the blockhouses, the sentinels in the trees would join in, firing on the backs of the Allied troops and causing many casualties. It was weeks before the Allied soldiers caught on to the system, and meanwhile their casualties were extremely high.

MacArthur knew virtually nothing of all this. He only visited from the front once or twice, and his reports from his staff were meager because they, too, seldom went to the front line. They had underestimated the strength and determination of the Japanese all the way, and MacArthur could not believe the reports he received about the strength of the Japanese defenses. He actually accused the Thirty-second Division of cowardice and forced the removal of its commanding officer, only to find that the people he sent in did no better.

The liaison with the Australians was most imperfect. The operation was supposed to be cooperative, but General Sir Thomas Blamey, the Australian commander, was constantly bypassed and not asked for advice, although he was titularly field commander and knew the troops, the enemy, and the terrain far better than the Americans. MacArthur was determined to turn the Southwest Pacific operation—his command—into an American show.

From the beginning of his sojourn in Australia, MacArthur was unhappy with the U.S. command structure in the Pacific, and in this he was quite justified. The sensible thing to do, as the Allies did finally in Europe, was to create a supreme command. MacArthur said so, not once but many times, but since he was known for his enormous ego, that advice was lost in the distrust of the navy and of many of MacArthur's army associates, and the advice was not heeded. Instead a divided command was established, with MacArthur responsible for the Australian area and Admiral Chester W. Nimitz in command of all the rest of the Pacific. Also the navy war plan was followed in the beginning, which called for the drive to Japan to go through the Central Pacific. This was almost immediately nullified when Admiral Ernest J. King, the commander of the navy, realized in the summer of 1942 that the Japanese were completing an airfield on Guadalcanal Island in the Solomons that would give them air control of northern Australia. To stop this adventure, Admiral King ordered the invasion of Guadalcanal by the reinforced First Marine Division. MacArthur opposed the idea as foolhardy and bound to fail. He wanted the resources thus used to be sent to him, whereupon he would defeat the Japanese in New Guinea and then attack them at Rabaul, he said.

After months of tribulation the Guadalcanal invasion succeeded, and the Pacific command, now tactically under Vice Admiral William F. Halsey, moved on up the Solomons chain to New Georgia and then to Bougainville, just south of Rabaul. Meanwhile General MacArthur's command had been gaining strength and moving along in New Guinea. The Fifth Air Force was made into a powerful fighting machine. In the battle of the Bismarck Sea in the spring of 1943 the Fifth Air Force completely disrupted a Japanese convoy bound for New Guinea, and thereafter the Japanese did not again try to reinforce their troops by convoy. They had already gone on the defensive with the evacuation of Guadalcanal in February 1943 and the establishment by Imperial General Headquarters of a new defensive perimeter that envisaged the fall of Rabaul.

The Papua campaign was one of the costliest victories the Allies ever won in terms of casualties for the number of troops involved, far greater than the casualty percentages on Guadalcanal. The Australians suffered two-thirds of the brunt, but were given scant credit by the MacArthur command.

In the middle of 1943 MacArthur still wanted to invade Rabaul, which would have been the bloodiest battle yet, for General Harukichi Hyukatake had 100,000 troops available to defend. MacArthur's moves were devised for the ultimate invasion. After the Papua campaign he sent the Australians marching up the east coast of New Guinea to Finschhafen, where they had to be supported by the infant Seventh Fleet Amphibious Command because the terrain was so rugged. He also invaded Woodlark and Kiriwina islands. Woodlark Island is 200 miles south of Bougainville. Kiriwina is 125 miles south of New Britain Island. Both islands were to become air bases for the assault on Rabaul.

The Woodlark invasion was carried out by the 112th Cavalry Regiment and a force of Navy Seabees who would build the airstrip. The Kiriwina invasion was made by the 158th Army Regimental Combat Team and the army engineers.

As it turned out, both invasions were little but good practice for the amphibious command, because the Japanese had never fortified these islands and the small garrisons were long gone.

The landings were made on June 22 and June 23, without trouble, and the engineers got down to building the airfields. Soon a fighter squadron was moved to Kiriwina, but it was not needed because the chain of events was moving too rapidly. Woodlark was never actually employed as an air base.

By the fall of 1943 Washington realized that a more experienced and capable commander was desirable for the Seventh Fleet. General MacArthur did not like Vice Admiral Arthur Carpender, the commander of the Seventh Fleet, an assessment in which he joined a number of naval officers who had suffered from Carpender's machinations. So in the fall of that year Vice Admiral Thomas C. Kinkaid was chosen to replace Carpender. Kinkaid had been commander of cruisers for the American force at the battle of the Coral Sea, then at Midway. He had commanded the *Enterprise* task force in the Guadalcanal area, and if the actions of that force were not brilliant, at least he had followed Halsey's directives faithfully. In November 1942 Kinkaid had gone to Alaska to assume command of the North Pacific Force fighting the Japanese in the Aleutian Islands and had served there for 10 months, supervising the recapture of Amchitka Island early in 1943 and the occupation of Attu in May, and then Kiska in August.

Admiral King made the appointment without consulting MacArthur, whose feathers were ruffled, as might have been expected, but then King told MacArthur the appointment had not actually been made, and would Kinkaid be acceptable? MacArthur's ego was assuaged, and he accepted.

Admiral Kinkaid arrived in Brisbane on November 23, 1943, with Admiral Halsey as escort. He found a naval unit badly disorganized. Rear Admiral Daniel S. Barbey's amphibious force had very little to do with the submarine commands, one of which was located on the far side of Australia at Perth. Adding to Kinkaid's troubles, he had two bosses, not one. MacArthur was the commander of the Southwest Pacific, and therefore Kinkaid reported to him. But when the Seventh Fleet had been created, Admiral King in Washington had kept control of it personally and it was not part of the Pacific Fleet, although until Kinkaid's arrival the Seventh Fleet had been dependent on the Pacific Fleet for the loan of ships for all its operations.

MacArthur still wanted a real navy, with battleships and carriers, but he was not to get it—a matter that caused him deep frustration. He was vexed by the fact that he was not running the Pacific war, which he thought he should be doing. He felt that the navy and General George C. Marshall were his enemies.

About the navy he was more than half right—the naval high command found MacArthur overly ambitious—but about Marshall there was not the slightest bit of evidence to support MacArthur's contention. Marshall was aware of MacArthur's quirks but did his best to keep aloof from personality problems.

Kinkaid set out to give MacArthur the best navy he could. One change—to a policy long followed in the Pacific Fleet—was to make the naval commander responsible for the amphibious operation until the troops were established ashore and the military commander had set up his command post. This eliminated one source of friction: the navy's feeling that it was simply being used to transport troops for the army.

MacArthur was still looking to the invasion of Rabaul, but also ahead to the jump-off for the Philippines. The master plan of 1944 called for MacArthur to invade Mindanao and move up the island chain and Nimitz to continue across the Central Pacific. After the Marianas invasion and the battle of the Philippine Sea, which devastated the Japanese carrier force, the Imperial General Staff began planning for the next expected American moves. They developed Operation Sho, which was designed to employ the remnants of the navy, the army and navy air forces, and the army ground forces to best advantage. It was obvious that the next big American operation had to be against a considerable land mass: the Philippines, Formosa, the China coast, or the Japanese homeland. Any of these operations would give the Japanese the chance to employ sea, air, and ground forces, and would reduce the Allied advantage because the Japanese land forces were still extremely strong.

After the men of the Australian Seventh Division marched up the Huon Peninsula against Finschhafen, Admiral Daniel S. Barbey, as commander of the Seventh Fleet Amphibious Corps, made preparations to land troops at Cape Gloucester on New Britain Island. This seemed to be a very important operation at the time. It would give MacArthur a base for an overland assault on Rabaul at the other end of the island, and MacArthur was convinced that Rabaul would have to be taken by force although the Joint Chiefs of Staff had already agreed that the base should be bypassed and left to wither.

However, the Joint Chiefs of Staff had second thoughts about that plan: If Admiral Halsey could secure air bases in the middle of Bougainville, without having to conquer the whole Japanese division stationed on that island, then the capture of other key points and the ringing of Rabaul with Allied air bases could destroy its air and seapower and leave those 100,000 Japanese troops stranded. This idea began to appeal more and more to the Joint Chiefs, although they did not know that the Japanese high command had already written off the South Pacific as indefensible and drawn the line at Borneo where the oil fields were, then up through the Philippines, and then around the inner empire and China coast.

To undertake the land attack, General MacArthur now had Lieutenant General Walter Krueger's Sixth U.S. Army, to which were added the men of the First Marine Division, who had fought so spectacularly at Guadalcanal. In April and May 1943 the men of the Fifth Marine Regiment were practicing assault landings on the beach at Port Phillip Bay near Melbourne. They were short of ships, but they were becoming familiar with the new techniques of amphibious warfare learned since their landings on Guadalcanal in August 1942.

Two other marine regiments, the Seventh Marines and the Seventeenth Marines, were also prepared for employment in this new MacArthur campaign, and all during the autumn they trained in amphibious operations.

Admiral Kinkaid's first major command problem was brought up in December. In past operations Admiral Barbey had been troubled by a lack of fighter air support from the Fifth Air Force at the critical hours of the actual landing of the troops. Kinkaid took this problem to MacArthur—something Admiral Carpender had been unable to do because of the bad relationship—and MacArthur promised the fullest cooperation from General Kenney.

In December the troops began to move to Cape Sudest, the point at which they would board vessels for the assault on New Britain. They were to land at Borghen Bay and then establish several beachheads. They were then assigned to capture the Cape Gloucester airfields.

One of these airstrips was finished and one had just been started by the Japanese. They were both located on the grassland near Borf Point, which was defended by the Japanese Seventeenth Army Infantry Division, since observation planes from Rabaul had been warning for weeks that attack by the Allies was imminent.

In the second week of December 12, 1943, scouts landed from PT boats at Rooke Island and Tolokawa Island and ascertained that the area was defended by about 1,200 troops.

The first point of attack was going to be Cape Merkus and three offshore islands, and the purpose was to cut off the barge traffic that ran along the inshore side of these islands, the way that the Japanese resupplied their troops in the whole area after the battle of the Bismarck Sea.

On December 5, 1943, a landing ship loaded up marine tractors and equipment, and a transport loaded its troops. Two destroyer transports, the *Sands* and the *Humphreys*, also loaded up for a practice landing. It was not very successful and revealed some gaps in training of junior officers.

D-Day was December 15 and the invasion force loaded up two days earlier at Goodenough. General MacArthur came down to watch two big ships, two destroyer transports, and many landing craft and amphibious tractors carried aboard for the actual landings. On December 14 the force set out, escorted by Rear Admiral V.A.C. Crutchley's Australian cruiser force and nine destroyers. The Japanese soon had word of it from their aerial observation planes and ordered an aerial attack launched at dawn on December 15.

The convoy reached its unloading area at 4 A.M., and an hour later the big ships had unloaded and started back for New Guinea. First came a group of rubber boats, then troops off the destroyers into landing craft. The intelligence officers wondered if the landings would be opposed but soon got their answer: The Japanese began firing machine guns and in a few minutes sank all but three of the rubber boats. The destroyer *Shaw* then began firing its five-inch guns, and the Japanese fire quieted down. The landings proceeded and by afternoon the beachhead was secure. The Americans discovered that about 120 Japanese had been defending there, and most of them escaped across the bay to New Britain Island.

The Japanese air attack arrived at about 8 A.M. The Americans had sent a squadron of P-38 fighter planes to protect the landings, and a squadron of Zeros arrived to challenge them. Altogether about 40 Japanese fighters and bombers attacked. But they did not have many targets; almost all the invasion ships had already left. They did blow up one *LCVP* Landing Craft, Vehicles and Personnel but the antiaircraft fire from the American-held beach soon discouraged the Japanese aircraft.

During the next week the Japanese continued to launch air attacks on the American beachhead, but American planes usually drove them off. By the end of three weeks there were no more attacks.

General Julian Cunningham, the commander of the 112th Cavalry, moved his command post ashore and began to send out patrols to see what Japanese opposition existed at the western end of New Britain. They saw many Japanese, but (it was hard to engage them.) The Japanese moved in barges in the shallow water and seemed very elusive. The Japanese made several attacks on the airfield area where the engineers were working but the Americans successfully resisted them.

On December 20 the troops again began rehearsing at Cape Sudest for more landings in the Cape Gloucester area, for MacArthur was sure this was the way to Rabaul.

From the Japanese point of view the war had gone completely topsy-turvy. A year earlier the Japanese had air superiority and the mastery of the seas in the South Pacific. But now it was all reversed, and the Fifth Air Force bombed and strafed Japanese installations at Rabaul every day and flew support to the MacArthur forces landed on the west end of the island. Starting on December 1 the bombers dropped tons of bombs in the Cape Gloucester area and knocked out the Japanese defenses there long before the troops were scheduled to land. The Japanese went into the jungle for safety as Admiral Barbey's amphibious forces readied themselves for the coming landings. On Christmas Eve the American troops were at sea, heading out from Cape Sudest, bound for New Britain.

Once more there were many questions in the minds of the invaders, but this force was more powerful than any MacArthur had yet been able to field, and they were commanded by Marine Major General William H. Rupertus of the First Marine Division.

So Cape Gloucester was taken, after some heavy fighting in the air, the sinking of the destroyer *Brownson*, and the disabling of the destroyer *Shaw* by Japanese bombers. By the evening of D-Day the Allies had 11,000 men ashore. There was hard fighting at places called Hill 660, Target Hill, Aogiri Ridge, and Suicide Creek. The Japanese suffered about 5,000 casualties, and after three days the Marines suffered about 50, half of them dead. By January 16 the battle was coming to a conclusion, and by the end of the month General Krueger reported that the western part of New Britain was securely in American hands. The Americans built up the airfields, but then the Joint Chiefs of Staff turned thumbs down on MacArthur's hope to attack Rabaul. The Central Pacific drive had succeeded very nicely. In November Nimitz's forces had taken the Gilbert Islands, and early in 1944 they had captured the Marshalls and were moving toward the Marianas. General MacArthur was still talking about making the Philippines the target of importance, but the best he could do with the Joint Chiefs of Staff was to get a commitment to support a landing in the southern Philippines, while the navy continued to lead the way with the Central Pacific drive.

By the end of February 1944 the marines had cleared the Japanese completely out of the western end of New Britain, and Cape Gloucester's airfields were completely safe and ready to be used. But by that time nobody cared. The Rabaul operation had been scrapped, and the eyes of the Americans were turned toward the Philippines and the Marianas. The navy expected to continue its drive, and MacArthur hoped—how he did not quite know—to manage to bring his troops into the forefront of the Pacific war.

CHAPTER THREE

The New War

In the beginning of 1944 it became clear in Washington that the war was moving more quickly, and favorably, than anyone would have expected a year earlier. The Central Pacific campaign was warming up to assault the Marianas Islands, which were needed for bases for the B-29s to bomb Japan. General MacArthur's forces were moving very satisfactorily up New Guinea, from which they would ultimately launch an invasion of the Philippines. The debate continued at command levels: Should the major approach be through the Philippines or Formosa? It was not settled that winter. The Joint Chiefs ordered Nimitz to continue in the Central Pacific and MacArthur to get ready to assault Mindanao.

The next big MacArthur move would be into Hollandia and bypass the Wewak area, where the Japanese had considerable strength. Indeed, at this point in the war, the Imperial General Headquarters in Tokyo was more concerned about MacArthur's operations than about those of Nimitz, and was shepherding its naval and air strength to stop MacArthur in New Guinea if the Japanese could do it.

As the Allies came closer to Japan the need for real cooperation between the Southwest Pacific command and the Pacific Ocean areas was evident, and on March 20, 1944, Admiral Nimitz paid a visit to Brisbane. The occasion was an invitation from MacArthur to talk about future operations. MacArthur needed the use of Nimitz's ships for some of his invasions, and Nimitz needed MacArthur's land-based air support to stage some of his forces into the Marianas.

The meeting was cordial; if the atmosphere was still strained because of the basic difference of approach of the two commands, Nimitz was very diplomatic and there were no ruffled feathers. Nimitz agreed to send a dozen of the fast carriers that had recently joined the Pacific Fleet to support the Hollandia operation, which was laid on in New Guinea for mid-April, but how long they could stay was another matter. MacArthur would have liked to have them around for a while but Nimitz did not want them kept in a static situation, where they were likely to attract Japanese torpedo bombers.

Three weeks before the Hollandia landings the fast carriers were out raiding Palau, and they eliminated Japanese air power there.

The Hollandia operation was a complete success and brought congratulatory messages from General Marshall and others. Scheduled were the assault on Wakde Island, Biak Island, Noemfoor Island, and Sansapoor. Wakde was scheduled for May 17 and Biak 10 days later. At Wakde the Allies found the Japanese entrenched in coral caves, and before the island was secured, 40 Americans and nearly 800 Japanese died.

But the heaviest Japanese concentrations were along the shoreline from Toem to Sarmi. Here 10,000 Japanese troops were dug in. An extra American division, the Sixth Division, was sent in to combat the Japanese Thirty-sixth Division, but the area was not secured until September, although the airfields were in use. In fact, the Japanese held on stubbornly in the area and were still in control at Sarmi at war's end, although they did not influence operations. Soon Wakde was supporting two heavy bomber groups, two fighter groups, and two reconnaissance squadrons to cover the future invasions and fly support for Nimitz's incursions up north. This area became an important staging point for the invasions of Biak, Morotai, and ultimately Leyte Gulf.

Biak was a different story. Admiral Soemu Toyoda, who became chief of the Japanese fleet after the death in a plane crash of Admiral Mineichi Koga, decided early in May that the time had come for the "decisive battle" against the American fleet. His A-Go plan called for Admiral Jisaburo Ozawa's First Mobile Fleet (the successor to the decimated Combined Fleet) to lure the Pacific Fleet to the Palau region, where Japanese carriers plus land-based aircraft would destroy the Americans. Toyoda saw that MacArthur was building air bases all the way up the New Guinea coast. If he could seize the Japanese bases in the Schouten Islands and Geelvink Bay, he could disrupt the A-Go operation. Therefore it was important that MacArthur be stopped right at Biak, the largest of the Schouten Islands. Imperial General Headquarters agreed that the security of the A-Go plan demanded the reinforcement of troops, aircraft, and the fleet. Colonel Naoyuki Kuzume, the commander at Biak, was warned to expect invasion and grouped his defenses in the caves above the island's three air bases. His defense plan called for control of the airstrips.

On May 27 the Seventh Fleet Amphibious Force arrived off Biak, expecting an easy victory over the estimated 2,000 Japanese defenders. First the air and naval forces staged an impressive bombardment but did not know that the Japanese were either inland or deep in caves. Then the Forty-first U.S. Division landed on beaches nine miles east of the airfield area. One regiment went along the beach and another pushed along the inland route among the hills. Both regiments were stopped short on May 29 by fierce fire from well-placed installations.

The advance was stalled until the 163rd Regimental Combat Team was rushed from Wakde, and the advance continued at a much slower pace. On June 7 the 186th Regiment captured the eastern air strip but the Japanese had built fields of fire onto the strip, and so the Americans were soon pinned down there. Planes could not use the field and the troops could not move. Admiral Kinkaid considered evacuating the troops by sea.

General MacArthur had been overconfident and on May 28 had made a statement that the impending victory at Biak meant the end of the New Guinea campaign. By June 3 he still did not seem to realize the facts and was talking about mopping-up operations, when actually his troops were fighting for their lives and the issue was very much in doubt.

By the end of the first week in June, it was apparent that the airfields would not be ready in time to give the help that MacArthur had promised Nimitz for the Marianas operation. General MacArthur demanded action from General Krueger, who considered relieving the commander of the Forty-first Division but awaited a report from his chief of staff, who had gone to Biak for a look. The chief of staff then reported that the Americans were having real trouble at Biak, but that the Forty-first Division seemed about to achieve victory.

The Americans did not know that the Japanese intended to make a real fight there.

They learned on June 13 when Major General Horace H. Fuller of the Forty-first Division informed General Krueger that the Japanese had landed reinforcing troops at Biak. Fuller said he needed another regiment, and Krueger agreed to send one from the Twenty-fourth Division. Krueger did not believe the story of the reinforcements, but it was true: The Japanese had landed 1,000 troops from barges.

General MacArthur demanded action, and so General Krueger relieved General Fuller and put General Robert Eichelberger, who had commanded the ground troops in the Buna campaign, in charge of the Biak operation. General Fuller was angry and said he did not intend to serve in the MacArthur theater again. He was moved to the Southeast Asia Command where he served ably as deputy chief of staff to Lord Mountbatten. Eichelberger appointed Brigadier General Jens A. Doe as commander of the Forty-first Division, but it soon became apparent that the problem had been addressed in a simplistic way. The Japanese continued to resist stoutly and prevented the use of any of the airstrips until June 22, when the first strip was secured. (The others were not ready until August, when Krueger declared the Biak operation to be ended. It had cost 400 Americans killed, 2,000 wounded, and 7,400 noncombatant casualties to kill 4,700 Japanese and capture 220.)

The Biak operation was also notable because the Japanese planned a vigorous attack on the Americans there, and early in June Japanese aircraft began to attack the Allied invasion fleet and damaged the cruiser *Nashville*. A Japanese reinforcement convoy headed for Biak, bringing 2,500 soldiers. The Americans sent a surge of airpower toward the Japanese forces. This Japanese attack was a part of Operation Kon, an intensive effort to defend Biak. But the air assault that was supposed to be decisive was crippled when the naval aviators, assembled from Central Pacific bases, began to come down with malaria. The runs from the Philippines to Biak by the navy were not very satisfactory.

The first Japanese convoy was aborted off the coast of the Vogelkap when Allied reconnaissance planes spotted it and began tracking it. At the same time the Japanese convoy commander had a report that the American fleet had arrived off Biak, so he turned about and sought safety.

The second Kon convoy was driven off several days later by Allied aircraft and a cruiser force under Admiral Crutchley on the night of June 8.

The third Kon reinforcement was intended to be decisive. Vice Admiral Matome Ugaki, who had been Admiral Isoroku Yamamoto's chief of staff and was now commander of Battleship Division Number One, assembled a huge expedition at Batjan in the Moluccas, which included the huge battleships *Musashi* and *Yamato*, as well as a strong force of cruisers, light cruisers, and many destroyers and escorts. Several thousand troops were riding in transports. The force was large enough to destroy Admiral Kinkaid's Seventh Fleet fighting force and to land a decisive number of troops at Biak.

But on June 11 as Admiral Ugaki was weighing anchor at Batje, Saipan radioed Tokyo that the island was under attack from an American armada. The naval authorities on the island warned of impending invasion. Admiral Toyoda then switched from the Kon plan to the A-Go plan, which called for a confrontation with the American fleet.

Admiral Jisaburo Ozawa then succeeded to command of the operation and Admiral Ugaki joined him in what became the battle of the Philippine Sea, in which the Japanese lost most of their aircraft and the carriers were either sunk or crippled so that the whole force retired. In the aftermath of the defeat, Operation Kon against New Guinea was forgotten.

So Biak was secured without a major battle. Then came the landings on Noemfoer in early July, and after that the campaign against the strong Japanese forces in the Vogelkap. A big fight was expected here, but the Japanese naval forces had moved to Lingga Roads at Singapore and the fight did not develop. The area was secured and air bases were built for the support of the coming attacks on Morotai and the Halmahera Islands, scheduled for September.

By mid-July General MacArthur's interest in the New Guinea campaign had succumbed to his greater interest in moving back to the Philippines. There were still many thousands of Japanese soldiers in Dutch New Guinea, but in correspondence with General Marshall, MacArthur said they were no threat and could be left to wither on the vine.

The last operation on the Vogelkap Peninsula began on July 30 when 7,300 troops of the Sixth Division landed at Sansapoor and Mar, about a hundred miles west of Manokwari, the Japanese Second Army's headquarters. Two airfields were built at Mar to serve the forthcoming Morotai operation. The Japanese had a division and three brigades in the area but did not oppose the landings or fight back. Later, only after MacArthur had moved on to the Philippines, the Japanese on New Guinea came back to life, and then the Australians had the task of rooting out the bypassed forces.

CHAPTER FOUR

Attack to the North

After Cape Gloucester the Allied plan of movement took a leap. General MacArthur and his naval chief, Admiral Thomas Kinkaid, commander of the Seventh U.S. Fleet, decided to bypass the Japanese bases remaining in British New Guinea and drive north to Dutch New Guinea, which was MacArthur's idea of the jumping-off place for the invasion of the Philippines.

By March 1944 the Allies had moved up New Guinea and had captured Manus Island and Seeadler Harbor, which was one of the finest naval anchorages in the world, capable of housing a whole fleet. The plan now put to the Joint Chiefs of Staff called for Admiral Halsey to seize Emirau Island. That move would complete the ring around Rabaul and make it unnecessary to attack the place. So that was done, and the Allies had no opposition—the Japanese had seen the future and had evacuated Emirau Island.

The Japanese at about this time decided to get out of Truk as part of their tightening of the perimeter of empire. They moved their Combined Fleet from Truk to the Palau Islands, and the major elements of that fleet to the anchorage at Tawitawi near the tip of Borneo, where the ships would be close to their fuel oil supply. They kept the fleet together as well as they could; part of it was stationed at Singapore, and part of it was in Japan, where some major ships had been sent for repair after the wearing battles of the Guadalcanal campaign. Although Admiral Mineichi Koga had replaced Admiral Yamamoto as commander of the Combined Fleet after Yamamoto was ambushed and killed by the Americans in the spring of 1943, the Japanese naval war plan was unchanged. More than before the Japanese navy now counted on one big naval battle to redress the growing odds against their victory. They knew that the Americans were getting more carriers, but they reasoned that since they held the islands of the Western Pacific, the Indies, and the Philippines, they could get along with fewer carriers.

The Joint Chiefs of Staff were having some second thoughts about the command situation in the Pacific. The crux would come with the next big invasion. So far, the Central Pacific campaign and even Guadalcanal and the South Pacific campaign of Admiral Halsey had demanded minimal numbers of troops and military hardware. But in a campaign in the Philippines, Formosa, China, and certainly Japan, the Allies would find themselves battling the Japanese Imperial Army, which had plenty of artillery, tanks, and heavy equipment.

Therefore the Pacific war was going to develop into a different kind of war, the sort that the army understood very well. Following the victory at Bougainville and the establishment bases at Empress Augusta Bay, the Joint Chiefs gave authority over the South Pacific to MacArthur, and Admiral Halsey closed down his Third Fleet headquarters at Noumea and moved back to Pearl Harbor and a fleet command that alternated with that of Admiral Raymond Spruance.

In addition, the American resources available to the Pacific had increased so much that the Seventh Fleet was now going to become a real fleet, no longer dependent as it had been in the past on the Nimitz organization to lend ships for invasions. It would have cruisers, destroyers, destroyer transports, cargo ships, landing ships, and landing craft. In other words, Admiral Kinkaid would now be independent of the Pacific Fleet for invasion operations.

All this came on the eve of the planning for the move into Dutch New Guinea, which was the preliminary to MacArthur's dream of returning victoriously to the Philippines.

CHAPTER FIVE

Heading for the Philippines

In mid-July 1944 General MacArthur's troops in New Guinea were fighting fierce battles with General Hatazo Adachi's force, which consisted of two full divisions and parts of two others. But Adachi did not commit his force to one objective; instead he fought piecemeal, and the Allied artillery made all the difference in such a situation. The fighting around Aitape continued through August but MacArthur paid little attention, leaving it all in the hands of General Krueger.

At first General MacArthur contemplated the advance only straight to Mindanao, as foreseen by the Joint Chiefs of Staff. He would first take the island of Halmahera for its air base potential, but the big jump to Mindanao would require many ships, and MacArthur did not have them. He sent emissaries to Pearl Harbor. After meetings with the Pacific Fleet staff, the Southwest Pacific staff made plans to capture Morotai and the Talaud Islands, which lie south at Mindanao, before hopping to Mindanao.

There was a big problem about Halmahera, too. The Japanese Second Army was there in force, with some 30,000 troops who could defend any and all of the landing beaches. On the other hand, Morotai was reportedly defended by only 1,000 Japanese and was only a few miles northeast of Halmahera. So MacArthur set up his schedule. Morotai would be invaded on September 15, the nearby Talaud Islands about October 15, and Mindanao about November 15.

Major General Charles P. Hall was assigned to command the Tradewinds Task Force that would assault the Pitoe area of southwest Morotai using 61,000 troops, most of whom were engineers and service personnel. The job would be to take the island quickly and then rush to build airfields to cover the invasions of the Talaud Islands and Mindanao. The Thirty-first Division would make the assault under Major General John C. Persons and would be carried to Morotai by Admiral Barbey's amphibious landing force. Rear Admiral Russell S. Berkey would manage the cruiser support group that would bombard the island and protect the landing force. For the first time the Seventh Fleet would have an air force of its own, so to speak. Six escort carriers under Rear Admiral Thomas L. Sprague would cover the landings, as would the planes of General Kenney's Fifth Air Force.

Admiral Halsey's Bougainville campaign had proved that on a large island it was not necessary to occupy the whole area, and this tactic would be repeated at Morotai. The Allies would concentrate on the Pitoe beachhead, which would be expanded into a 12-square-mile perimeter. In this area the airfields would be built.

General MacArthur decided that he would observe the Morotai landings, so on September 12 he had boarded the cruiser *Nashville* at Hollandia and the cruiser had moved out to join Admiral Berkey's support group. On September 15 the cruiser force bombarded Halmahera to hurt the Japanese enough that they would not try to mount a counteroffensive from the large land force on the island after the Americans landed on Morotai.

Then, about 8 A.M. on September 15, the landings began; two hours later MacArthur and Admiral Barbey went ashore. MacArthur observed that he would soon have an air base within 300 miles of the Philippines, and by 1 P.M. the general was back aboard the *Nashville* and heading for Brisbane to continue the planning for the invasion of the Philippines.

Morotai turned out to be even more lightly defended by the Japanese than anticipated. Only 400 enemy soldiers were found there, and the occupation was a simple matter for the 20,000 troops.

That same morning in September Admiral Nimitz's Central Pacific forces invaded the Palau Islands and were met with heavy opposition that would last for many weeks. Major General William H. Rupertus's First Marine Division at Peleliu faced more than 11,000 entrenched and vigorous Japanese. The Japanese fought to the death, but before they were wiped out at the end of November, they had caused 6,500 marine casualties, the highest casualty rate in any assault in American history. Ironically, because of changes in the general war picture, Peleliu, which was to have played a major role in the assault on the Philippines, played no part at all.

On September 23 Major General Paul J. Mueller's Eighty-first Army Division attacked the island of Ulithi, having taken the island of Angaur. They found it totally undefended, and so without effort they had secured one of the finest harbors in the world, just north of Yap Island, a harbor that would in the next few weeks play a major role in the invasion of the Philippines.

Now the work began in earnest. MacArthur spent most of the time in Brisbane. Two plans were developed: One, Musketeer I, was for the invasion of Mindanao. The second, Musketeer II, was for the invasion of Luzon Island.

As General MacArthur was making these plans, the debate was still going on in Washington: the Philippines or Formosa? Admiral King stood for Formosa, and the Joint Chiefs were almost deadlocked on the issue. President Roosevelt had been much impressed by MacArthur's arguments at the July meeting in Hawaii, and in September the decision was finally made: the Philippines. Mindanao would be invaded in November and Leyte in December, and then Luzon early in 1945.

But none of this was decided even by early September. Admiral King was still arguing for an invasion of Formosa by the Pacific Fleet forces to come at about the same time as the MacArthur move against Mindanao. Generals Marshall and Air Force Chief H. H. Arnold were delaying decisions, largely because of the progress of the war in Europe. There was some indication that the war there might end before the the year was out. This change would enable the United States to concentrate enormous forces against Japan. Marshall and Arnold actually preferred the Formosa plan to the Philippine plan, but if all those resources were available, they might be able to do both simultaneously. Admiral William D. Leahy, the President's military assistant, cast his vote with Arnold and Marshall against making plans further than the Mindanao operation. So, as the second week of September began, the future course of the Pacific war was still undecided.

CHAPTER SIX

Divided Commands

To begin with, General Eichelberger was there first. Lieutenant General Robert L. Eichelberger arrived in the Southwest Pacific in August 1942 to find that the American troops recently moved into the theater were very much a mixed bag. The Thirty-second and Forty-first divisions were both National Guard units, bolstered with draftees, and neither had adequate combat training by that summer when they were supposed to go into action. Eichelberger hoped to command the American troops in the field, in MacArthur's September offensive against Buna and Gona, but he ran afoul of MacArthur's chief of staff, General Richard K. Sutherland, who saw that he was frustrated at every turn until the Allied troops got mired down. Eichelberger sent the Thirty-second Division into action. Because their training was still incomplete and they faced extremely confident and experienced Japanese defenders in the Buna-Gona areas, they feared high losses without gaining ground. By the last week in November the Americans were hopelessly stuck. Misreading the situation from poor staff reports, MacArthur sent Eichelberger to take command of the American troops and relieve General Edwin F. Harding, commander of the division. Eichelberger did. Eichelberger also remembered MacArthur's statement to him, "I want you to take Buna, or not come back alive."

Eichelberger replaced men right and left and made many mistakes, but eventually the Australians brought up reinforcements and the Americans learned jungle fighting by doing it.

When the campaign ended Eichelberger received some honors including the Distinguished Service Cross, but so did some of MacArthur's staff who had not been near the Japanese. He had violated the only rule that mattered to MacArthur: He had gotten much publicity in America for his conduct of operations in New Guinea, and MacArthur's ego could not stand that. In a sidelong way MacArthur threatened Eichelberger with demotion to colonel and return to the United States, and thereafter Eichelberger shied away from any publicity.

The command problem became serious because Lieutenant General Walter Krueger of the Sixth Army outranked Eichelberger, and in any event there was no real need for two lieutenant generals in command responsibility for the number of troops involved.

In 1943 the problem of two bulls in one pasture was uncomfortably solved when MacArthur put Eichelberger in charge of the First Army Corps, which turned out to be a training unit for the Twenty-fourth, Thirty-second, and Forty-first divisions. Eichelberger had vowed to himself that he would never again lead untrained troops in combat and had so impressed MacArthur with his tales of the difficulties of the untrained troops that he got the assignment with the First Army Corps—not glamorous, but absolutely essential to the American war effort.

Indeed, it was Eichelberger's reports to MacArthur that brought General Krueger to the Southwest Pacific. He was so impressed by the lack of training of the troops he had been sent that he asked Washington to send General Krueger, who then headed the U.S. Third Army at San Antonio.

Krueger might well have been a German general in this war were it not for the vagaries of fate. His father had been a Prussian officer in the army of the kaiser, but after he died in 1885, when Krueger was four years old, his mother brought him and two younger children to live with relatives in the United States. Krueger had first joined the service in the Spanish-American War and had worked his way through the ranks. He was a real soldier's soldier. By 1941 he had been promoted to lieutenant general and was regarded as one of the most effective field officers in the army.

MacArthur asked for Krueger and the Third Army for two reasons. One was that he was impressed with Krueger as a general. The second was that MacArthur did not like sharing authority or responsibility, and the Southwest Pacific command was supposed to be a joint command, with General Sir Thomas Blamey in charge of ground forces. To isolate the Australians MacArthur decided to bring in an American army, which would be in a different chain of command. When Krueger reached the Southwest Pacific, in command of the new Sixth Army rather than the experienced Third Army, he was informed that he would be commanding "the Alamo Force."

Krueger then succeeded Eichelberger as the senior field commander and began to devote his efforts in the winter of 1943 to the ultimate reduction of Rabaul, which was then the objective of the Joint Chiefs of Staff for the Southwest Pacific.

Personally Eichelberger and Krueger got on well. They shared a distaste for General Sutherland, MacArthur's chief of staff.

It was General Krueger who carried out the MacArthur battle plans for 1943—Kiriwina and Woodlark islands, then Cape Gloucester, and the other points that encircled Rabaul. The Sixth Army had led the drive up the northern coast of New Guinea, that series of assaults described later in this book. By the end of the summer of 1944, the Japanese had been either defeated or isolated on New Guinea.

Meanwhile, General Eichelberger spent 1943 training the troops for battle, and in January 1944 he was selected to command the Hollandia invasion forces with 37,000 combat troops. The actions at Tanahmerah Bay and Humboldt Bay were successful. But hardly had Eichelberger begun to relax after the successful Hollandia operation than MacArthur sent for him and asked him to salvage the Biak operations, which had gone astray in the Allied failure to understand the Japanese reaction to Biak and their decision to mount a strong defense there in Operation Kon. Eichelberger solved the problem in a week by correctly assessing the nature of the Japanese defenses and enveloping the Japanese defense lines, thus ensuring his designation as MacArthur's "fireman"—the man called upon to relieve an emergency.

General MacArthur was so impressed by Eichelberger's tactical talents that in the summer of 1944 he rewarded him with command of a new army, the Eighth U.S. Army. The staff of the Eighth Army was then on its way to Hollandia. Eichelberger met them there and took over the Eighth Army on September 9. In this new command he was back in the training business for the next few months while General Krueger ran the initial operations in the assault on the Philippines.

In the late summer of 1944 General Krueger and his staff were planning the Mindanao landings with Major General Stephen J. Chamberlin, MacArthur's operations officer. Colonel Clyde D. Eddleman and other officers on Krueger's staff were unhappy with the MacArthur staff's optimistic attitude toward building airfields on Leyte to support the landings. The plan called for the building of fields to accommodate two fighter groups, one bomber group, and seven additional squadrons within five days after the landings. Colonel Eddleman said it was an impossible task. The invasion day would be in the middle of the rainy season and typhoons had to be expected. But the MacArthur staff was not listening and decided to proceed as planned with the program.

CHAPTER SEVEN

Changes

After the devastating battle of the Philippine Sea in which the Japanese naval aviation carrier fleet had been decimated by plane, pilot, and carrier loses, the Imperial Japanese Navy had developed a desperation project—the Sho (Victory) Operation.

The Sho plan was to be put into effect at the moment it became clear the Allies were launching a new major invasion effort within the empire. For this purpose the empire consisted of the Philippines, Formosa, and the Japanese islands themselves. In that summer of 1944, since the Americans themselves did not know where they were going to land next, it was inconceivable that the Japanese should be able to guess, but they had all the major possibilities covered. If and when the Allies moved, the Japanese navy would respond with a last major strike using all its resources: This strike would also be carried out by the army and the army air forces.

One day in August several members of Admiral Toyoda's staff came down from Japan to Lingga Roads, just outside Singapore, to visit with Vice Admiral Takeo Kurita. Kurita commanded the southern element of the Combined Fleet, the battleships and cruiser force, which had been kept near the Borneo fuel supply because of the chronic shortage of fuel oil in Japan. They talked to Kurita about the coming operation in which he was expected to play a major role.

They laid out the battle plan for Kurita: In case of Allied action he was to move swiftly to counter, with a major strike of the battle elements of the Japanese fleet. This would be supported by a separate movement of the air forces, which would be used to bait the enemy into attacking them, and thus draw the attention of the most important element of the American fleet, the carrier force, while the Japanese battleships and heavy cruisers got in among the landing forces and destroyed them.

By September 8 the Joint Chiefs of Staff were still debating the next major move against Japan. General MacArthur had never wavered in his advice that the Americans should move against the Philippines, but the Joint Chiefs were not sure. Still, time was wasting, so on that day they issued orders that the attack on Mindanao on November 15 would be followed by one on Leyte on December 20. Further than that they would not commit the resources; they spoke of securing Manila by February 20 or Formosa or Amoy on the coast of China by March 1, 1945. These latter were not plans, but hopes.

On that same day that the Joint Chiefs were talking in Washington, Admiral Halsey was afloat in the Pacific and launching air attacks against the Palau and adjacent islands, which were supposed to be heavily defended by Japanese air forces. They did find many planes but a sluggish defense that allowed them to destroy many on the ground. The next day and the next, Halsey sent his aircraft against Mindanao. In the next two days he made far-reaching raids against the central Philippines. What was apparent to him at the end of the five days of fighting was that the Japanese were not responding with anything like their old vigor.

On September 13 a pilot was rescued from Leyte Island where he had made an emergency landing the day before. He reported that the Filipinos said there were no Japanese at all on the island.

Based on his findings in the air sweep, Halsey sent a message to Admiral Nimitz recommending that the operations against the Talaud Islands and Mindanao be abandoned and the Allies strike straight for Leyte soon.

The high command had estimated that a major assault would have to be made against the Palau Islands, and the attack force was already at sea. Nimitz was not quite sure that the assault still would not be necessary so he refused to call it back, but the rest of the planned moves for the next months were scrapped and a whole new plan evolved to hit the Central Philippines hard and soon.

This was done very quickly. Nimitz received the information and recommendations from Halsey and immediately sent them to the Joint Chiefs of Staff. The Joint Chiefs were then meeting with Winston Churchill and the British chiefs of staff at Quebec, and they asked MacArthur for his views. MacArthur was just then aboard the *Nashville* heading for Morotai, and the cruiser was observing radio silence. So the MacArthur staff accepted the changes in his name, and a few hours later the Joint Chiefs ordered the changes, canceling the Talaud, Mindanao, and Yap operations.

The Leyte attack would be made on October 20, with General MacArthur providing the assault force and the Seventh Fleet providing transport and protection, while the Nimitz Pacific Fleet would support the operation with air strikes and naval action as needed. Nimitz would turn over to MacArthur on loan the Third Amphibious Force and the Twenty-fourth Army Corps.

When MacArthur learned of the changes he was delighted. Six days later—September 21—MacArthur informed the Joint Chiefs that he would be able to make his invasion of Luzon by December 20 instead of in 1945. The navy was still talking about the invasion of Formosa, but that could not occur until February, and it was important to keep the Japanese off balance, so the timing of the Luzon operation was just right.

Nimitz began planning a concurrent attack against Amoy on the China coast and Formosa, and as the planners considered the two-prong operation, they realized it would be enormously costly in terms of men needed.

MacArthur was now ebullient and promised to conquer Luzon in four to six weeks, apparently without knowing much about the Japanese strength in the islands, for when war's end came in August 1945, General Tomoyuki Yamashita was still fighting on Luzon.

Still, in September 1944 the MacArthur prognosis seemed sound enough, for the full fury of the Japanese beleaguered in their inner empire had not yet been felt. To be sure, the "fight to the death" traditions had been honored on Guadalcanal, at Buna, and elsewhere, but as the Allies approached Japan itself the Japanese will to resist became fanatical.

In September the Formosa versus Philippines issue suddenly evaporated. The major reason was a Japanese offensive in central and southeast China that threatened all the American air bases there and the Chinese regulars and irregulars who had been counted on to assist the Allied invasion. So the China part of the navy plan died, and when China no longer looked appealing, the need to invade Formosa evaporated, because the Formosa seizure was to be accomplished to back up the China invasion. At one time General Arnold had looked with favor on the Formosa venture because of the good B-29 bases the big island would afford. But the buildup of the bases in the Marianas obviated the need of the air force for Formosa.

Therefore by the end of September 1944 the Formosa and China plans were put on the shelf and the navy began thinking about Iwo Jima, which the air force wanted as a fighter base for the planes that could accompany the B-29s on the Japan raids, and Okinawa, which was to be a launching pad for the invasion of the Japanese home islands.

Admiral King was most reluctant to give up the China-Formosa invasion plan, at least partly because he did not want to relinquish control of the drive against Japan, which the navy had held since Guadalcanal. But Nimitz did not see how he could carry out the plan with the forces available to him and so said, which tipped the scales against Admiral King, and finally King agreed to table the Formosa plans on October 3. The new agreed-upon program called for

MacArthur to attack Luzon on December 20 and for Nimitz to attack Iwo Jima on January 20 and Okinawa on March 1.

Immediately after the Quebec decision of the Joint Chiefs of Staff the Southwest Pacific planners went into high gear. Admiral Kinkaid, Admiral Barbey, and General Krueger were all in Hollandia on a hillside overlooking Lake Sentani. MacArthur and his staff were only half a mile away. On September 17 Vice Admiral Theodore S. Wilkinson arrived, true to Nimitz's promise to give him the Third Amphibious Command, to share the Leyte responsibilities with Barbey Wilkinson would bring the Twenty-fourth Corps to Leyte. Admiral Barbey had the most frantic job, for his troops were scattered all over the Southwest Pacific, some of then in the Admiralty Islands, and some of their landing craft had not yet arrived from Pearl Harbor.

Because of the difficulties a number of troops would travel by LST, and that meant they would have to leave Manus Island by October 4.

The question of command of the amphibious operation was a sensitive one. Barbey, as commander of amphibious operations for the MacArthur theater, expected to have the command. But that presented complications because he was junior to several other admirals, including Wilkinson, who was a vice admiral while Barbey was only a rear admiral. The problem was solved by giving Admiral Kinkaid overall command of the naval forces in the operation, and he would cooperate with Admiral Halsey, who was bringing the Third Fleet to support the operation. Admiral Barbey would command part of the landing force.

The Southwest Pacific command put the number of Japanese on Leyte at 21,000. Perhaps an equal number of reinforcements could be expected from Mindanao and other islands after the Allies landed. MacArthur then decided to employ his two corps—two divisions from each—in the assault with a two-division reserve. This meant an invasion force of 133,000 troops plus 70,000 special troops.

The immediate problem, as seen from Southwest Pacific Headquarters, was to seize Leyte and control the Surigao

Strait to the south of it, and then with this as a springboard, to move farther into the Philippines. The landing area would be on the east coast of the island, between the towns of Tacloban and Dulag, which had about a half dozen airstrips to be captured and repaired. From these fields General Kenney's Fifth Air Force hoped to be operating in a matter of hours, thus freeing the navy aircraft carriers for other duties.

Admiral Kinkaid's reinforced fleet consisted of some 700 vessels. Still Kinkaid expected Admiral Halsey to pave the way for him by containing or destroying the Japanese fleet if it should appear; by scouring the Formosa, Luzon, Visaya, and Mindanao ares for warships and aircraft; by destroying ground defenses and installations with air strikes; and by providing direct support of the landing and following operations.

Admiral Nimitz did not believe the Japanese would take the Leyte attack lying down and was ready for a direct confrontation with the Japanese fleet. If such an opportunity presented itself, he told Admiral Halsey in his orders, Halsey was to make the destruction of the Japanese fleet his primary task. Halsey agreed wholeheartedly; he was particularly eager to destroy the Japanese carriers.

There were three task forces. A special task group consisted of the fleet flagship *Wasatch* and the light cruiser *Nashville*, which would carry General MacArthur. This group would have four destroyers and should be able to defend itself from air attack during the operations.

Task Group 77.2 was the bombardment and fire support group of the fleet. It consisted of six old battleships, all survivors of the Pearl Harbor attack. They were too slow to keep up with the carriers and cruisers but ideal for this task at Leyte. Rear Admiral Jesse B. Oldendorf also had in this group three heavy cruisers, four light cruisers, and 21 destroyers.

The covering force, Task Group 77.3, was commanded by Admiral Berkey again. It consisted of the cruisers *Phoenix, Boise, Australia*, and *Shropshire*, and seven destroyers.

An element that would become most important in this action was Task Group 77.4, commanded by Rear Admiral Thomas L. Sprague, which consisted of 16 escort carriers, with nine destroyers and 12 destroyer escorts. Altogether, these ships could be put together to make a battle force if that was necessary. Besides them there were the minesweepers, beach demolition groups, and service ships, and then Task Force 78 and Task Force 79. Task Force 78 was Admiral Barbey's landing force, which would land the Tenth Army Corps south of the Tacloban airport. Task Force 79 was Admiral Wilkinson's force, known as the southern attack force. It was to land its troop of the Twenty-fourth Corps between the small cities of San Jose and Dulag. Before the task forces would land their troops, however, the plan called for the seizure of several islands in the Surigao Strait area to prevent interference with the landings.

CHAPTER EIGHT

October Uncertainties

After the invasion of the Marianas Islands by the Americans in June 1944 the Japanese high command revised its overall defense strategy. The Imperial General Headquarters knew that a major battle was shaping up and welcomed it as a last desperate gamble through which they might win the single big victory that Yamamoto had said was necessary to bring America to the conference table. The Japanese were still operating in the shadow of Yamamoto, for what other hope could they have? They had begun to realize, even if dimly, that the admiral had been right in his appraisal of the productive capacity of American industry as the deciding factor in the Pacific war. What they did not realize even yet was that the American productive capacity had outstripped the Japanese capacity to change matters, even by success in one great battle. With some 20 carriers and dozens of escort carriers available, the Americans could lose 10 carriers in a battle and still proceed with the carrier war.

The new policy devised by Combined Fleet Commander in Chief Soemu Toyoda was given four designations, but the essence was the same in all of them. The total remaining naval resources of Japan would be flung into the battle, and it would demand the fullest cooperation of the navy land-based air fleets and the army and the army air forces. Generically the operations were called the Sho (Victory) Operation. Their numerical designations indicated the chances the Japanese high command gave of each operation materializing, except that Toyoda believed the chances of the Taiwan Ryukyus operation were most likely.

Sho 1—The Philippines
Sho 2—Taiwan and the Ryukyus (Okinawa)
Sho 3—Japanese home islands
Sho 4—Hokkaido and the Kurile Islands.

In preparation, that summer of 1944, the Japanese navy reorganized the land-based air forces, creating the Second Air Fleet under Admiral Shigeru Fukudome. This air fleet brought together many of the best remaining air units of the Imperial Navy. The air groups were placed along the line that runs from Kyushu, the southernmost home island, to the Ryukyus and Taiwan. The First Air Fleet, assigned to the Philippines, was also very strong, as was the Third Air Fleet, which was assigned the homeland area. The Second Air Fleet was assigned 510 land-based planes; the First Air Fleet, 350 planes; and the Third Air Fleet, 300 planes, since it was deemed not very likely that this attack would take place at this time. But as it turned out, not all the planes were available and the shortage of properly trained pilots was even worse. Japan was now paying dearly for its failure to increase pilot education as the Americans had done during the early days of the war. Besides the land-based air forces the navy still had about a hundred carrier planes left, even after the debacle in the battle of the Philippine Sea.* Added to that force were the Twelfth Air Fleet in Hokkaido and the Thirteenth Air Fleet in the Dutch East Indies. But these were scarcely considered in the weighting of the forces.

The Japanese Imperial Army announced that it was allocating 600 aircraft to the Sho Operation, 200 each in the first three possible areas of operation. This figure in no

*For an account of that battle, see Hoyt's *To the Marianas*.

way represented the army's potential; army and navy leaders had never gotten along very well and the army was not about to commit all its resources to a naval battle plan.

All during that summer of 1944 the Japanese had watched warily as the Americans built up their forces in the Southwest Pacific and the Central Pacific. They saw General MacArthur's steady movement up the Vogelkap and knew exactly what he proposed to do for he had told the world. But would the Americans support that plan?

The Japanese naval high command vacillated in their opinions. For a time they said it would be Okinawa but by early September the betting was on the Philippines, and Admiral Fukudome moved his headquarters of the Second Air Fleet from the Kanoya Air Base in Kyushu to the Takao Air Base in South Taiwan. Hurriedly Imperial General Headquarters also gave Fukudome command over all army air force units on Taiwan, which added another 200 planes to his command, but as he said, it was not much help because the army fliers were very badly trained by naval standards. All the Taiwan air bases were refurbished and Fukudome began planning to move his air units to the island. But he did not move quite fast enough.

Early in October 1944 Admiral William F. Halsey set out from Ulithi with elements of his Third Fleet. His task in the next few weeks would be not only to support the landing of General MacArthur's forces in the Philippines, but also to keep a sharp eye out for the Japanese fleet, which was expected to put up a final battle, and if possible to destroy that fleet. It might have been done the previous summer, when the American and Japanese fleets met in the battle of the Philippine Sea. But Admiral Spruance had refused to go after the Japanese fleet at that time. After the successful Marianas operations ended Spruance was roundly criticized at Pearl Harbor, particularly but not entirely by airmen, for his timidity, and one of the results of the discussions was insertion into the orders given Admiral Halsey by Admiral Nimitz that if he had chance to go after the Japanese fleet, that would become his primary obligation.

And so with four carrier task groups and a total of 17 fleet carriers and light carriers, Admiral Halsey was going hunting for the Japanese fleet. One of his first moves, on October 9 was to send a group of heavy cruisers and destroyers to bombard Marcus Island. That diversionary attack did not impress the Japanese, but something else did. On that same day a Japanese long-range patrol plane from Kanoya Air Base disappeared east of Okinawa. Actually the bomber was shot down by an American patrol bomber that had nothing to do with Halsey's operations, but the commander reported the loss to the Sasebo naval district, whose commander was very edgy and jumped to the conclusion that the bomber had been destroyed by planes from an American carrier task force.

The next morning, October 10, the American task force hit Okinawa. The Japanese were totally unprepared. There were no planes actually on the island air bases for protection, and by the time planes arrived from Kyushu the Americans were waiting for them and claimed to have shot down 111 Japanese aircraft. Almost as soon as the attack on Okinawa began, Admiral Toyoda, who was on Taiwan at the time, ordered the alert for Sho 2. The big American invasion, he said, was obviously going to come against Taiwan, so the fleet was alerted. But then at his Japan headquarters his chief of staff, Admiral Kusaka, had second thoughts. There was a great deal of activity in the south that might mean operations against the Philippines, so the order was given to be on the alert for Sho 1 as well as Sho 2. This was a little difficult since ships could not head in two directions at once. All they could do for the moment was load with fuel, supplies, and ammunition, and wait. But the Japanese navy now began to move. Admiral Kusaka also ordered all the remaining Japanese aircraft carriers to stand by and prepared to transfer their aircraft to land bases. Admiral Toyoda, who had been on his way back to Tokyo from a quick trip to the Philippines to assess the situation there, decided to stay on Taiwan and direct the coming battle from there.

On October 11, to prevent the Japanese from shuttling planes back down from the Philippines to help in the Taiwan fight, two of Admiral Halsey's task groups sent air strikes against Aparri airfield in the Philippines. This was done, but the results were less than spectacular: 15 planes destroyed as against seven lost in the operation.

Admiral Fukudome then had two extra days in which to prepare for the coming air attacks on Taiwan, but he did not use them very well. By the morning of October 12 he had transferred only about a hundred fighters from the Kyushu airfields to Taiwan's airfields of Takao and Shinchiku and 10 flying boats to Toko seaplane base. The other units of the Second Air Fleet were still not prepared to move.

But Halsey was.

On the afternoon of October 11 three escort carriers brought up 61 replacement aircraft to the carriers of Task Force 38, and that afternoon the ships refueled and headed for the launching point, where at dawn they would send the aircraft off to begin the battle.

At dawn on October 12 the American task force was about 90 miles off Taiwan. They expected an attack because they had been snooped the following evening and the Japanese knew their position. Late in the afternoon of October 11 Admiral Fukudome, expecting battle, had ordered all the aircraft on Taiwan except fighers and reconnaissance planes to be moved to Kyushu or concealed.

The 230 fighter planes on the island were divided into two groups, one scheduled to attack incoming aircraft above Takao and the other to defend Taihoku, the capital of the island. Admiral Fukudome also ordered his Special T Attack Force, in which he had supreme confidence, to launch its planes from its base in Kyushu to make night attacks against the enemy carrier groups at sea. Also all other units stationed on Kyushu were ordered to make night attacks on October 12 against the carriers, using the Ryukyu Islands as refueling bases.

The T Attack Force was Fukudome's primary hope for swift and complete victory over the Americans. The concept was almost half a century old, dating from the time after the Russo-Japanese War when Japanese naval feeling ran high against the United States for depriving Japan of cash from Russia in the Treaty of Portsmouth. The feeling had reached the stage that the navy had claimed the United States and not Russia was the primary enemy of the future. Therefore a naval strategy for war against the Americans had to be developed, and out of it came the plan to lure the Americans into Japanese waters and then destroy their fleet. It was called the "offensive-defensive" strategy, and it was anticipated that the great battle would take place at night. For this the Japanese then trained in every aspect on the sea, underneath it, and in the air. Particularly did the Japanese also esteem their submarine fleet for this purpose. They envisaged submarines attacking and inflicting attrition on the American fleet all the way across the Pacific. So imbued did the high command become with this concept that they ignored the lessons taught by the Germans in two wars that the primary use of the submarine in war is as commerce destroyer.

The T Attack Force then was the result of this application to air, and Admiral Fukudome was one of its staunchest advocates. The TAF had one other peculiarity: It was the only unit composed half of navy and half of army air force elements.

The army air forces had been difficult to deal with. For many years their war plan envisaged land warfare against the USSR and their air force was tailored accordingly with many short-range aircraft for tactical troop support. But after the China war began the army discovered it could not carry out bombing missions in the beginning because it did not have any aircraft capable of flying the 600 miles from Kyushu to the fighting front. So the army began to build a medium bomber, the Ki-81, modeled after the navy's twin-engined torpedo bombers. They finally had an aircraft that with auxiliary fuel tanks could travel 800 miles. The army had still balked at working with the navy until their refusal had been one of the major causes—as far as the navy was concerned—for the defeat at the Marianas. Then army policy reluctantly was changed. For training purposes they placed a squadron of Ki-81 planes under the TAF, but in the middle of training Imperial General Headquarters stepped in and ordered the army unit to become a part of the TAF. Later another squadron of army planes was added. The trouble was that the standard of training of the army pilots was not up to that of the navy pilots. The army pilots had to be specially instructed in over-water flight, and by the fall of 1944 the army pilots had only minimal skills of ocean navigation and training that had lasted from two to six months. The navy men in the T Attack Force were very distrustful of the abilities of their army comrades. As would be shown soon enough one of the principal failings of the army pilots was their inability to recognize and differentiate between types of ships. But the fact was that by 1944 the naval air force had lost so many experienced men that the naval T Attack Force was not much better than the army. Admiral Fukudome once went down the line of a group of pilots and asked how many had ever seen a submarine. Most had not. Still Fukudome set great store by his T Attack Force.

The name T Attack Force was chosen because T was the first letter of "typhoon," that most ferocious of storms for which the Japanese had enormous respect. This force had been trained in night operations and bad weather. It was made up of torpedo attack planes.

The commander of the group was Captain Shizuo Kuno, a veteran aviator, and the crew members were all veteran fliers. The force was organized in March 1944 and first attached directly to Imperial General Headquarters but then turned over to Admiral Fukudome's command.

On the morning of October 12 the battle began over Taiwan. An hour before sunrise a fighter sweep was launched, and hundreds of planes headed for Taiwan. Admiral Fukudome was confident of victory that morning. He was sure the number of planes he could put up, 230, would exceed the number that the Americans could launch from their carriers. Second, the Japanese were on home ground and their planes could land and refuel and fight again easily. He estimated the odds at 6:4 for the Japanese. But what happened was a terrible shock to the admiral. He watched from his command post in a cave above Takao airfield as a huge aerial combat began over the airfield. At first he saw the Japanese planes hurtling to intercept, and then he saw planes falling and assumed that they were enemy planes, but he soon discovered that the falling aircraft were Japanese. He noticed then, too, that the Japanese planes flamed as soon as they were hit while the enemy planes did not.

On this first day of the battle Fukudome realized that his fighter force was no match for the Americans, but he still had great faith in the T Attack Force.

In that first fierce battle the Japanese lost a third of their Taiwan fighter force. But that day the Americans flew 1,378 sorties from the four carrier groups, and the second wave saw less resistance, with only about 70 Japanese fighters taking off, and doing virtually no damage to the enemy. By the time the third wave arrived, no Japanese fighters took off to meet them.

Meanwhile from Kyushu on October 12, the Second Air Fleet launched an offensive against the Americans and claimed to have hit two carriers. Admiral Fukudome was dubious.

The attack of the T Attack Force began on the night of October 12. About 30 twin-engined bombers took off from Kyushu at 7 o'clock that night and the raids went on until midnight, mostly against Admiral Gerald Bogan's carrier group. Several planes were shot down by the Combat Air Patrol, and others by antiaircraft fire. No carriers were damaged.

The task force arrived at dawn on October 13 at a launch point southeast of Formosa and began launching planes before sunrise. Not so many sorties were flown this second day, slightly fewer than 1,000, but they plastered the airfields once again and found new airfields built by the

Japanese for this operational defense. That night the carrier *Franklin* was attacked by four torpedo planes and one of them, catching fire, slithered across the flight deck in an impromptu crash landing, burst into full flame, and slid over the side. Two of the torpedoes narrowly missed the carrier, but she was basically unhurt.

On the second day of the battle the heavy cruiser *Canberra* took a torpedo and was badly damaged. The torpedo struck between her two firerooms, and both were flooded. She lost all power. Admiral Halsey could have ordered her scuttled but decided to save the ship and had it taken under tow by the *Wichita*.

Admiral Halsey had originally planned for only two days' operations off Taiwan, but to save the cruiser and protect her he set up a third day of attacks, Also on October 14, B-29s from the China airfields near Chengdu arrived to work over the Japanese installations, which helped the attackers a great deal.

On the night of October 14 the T Attack Force attacked again as it had done every night and put a torpedo into the cruiser *Houston*. She, too, lost all power. She was taken in tow by the cruiser *Boston*.

On Kyushu the pilots of the T Attack Force came back from their missions with most glowing reports of victory. Captain Kuno believed the reports and sent messages to Admiral Fukudome and Admiral Toyoda reporting the great events. So Imperial General Headquarters soon announced that Operation Sho 2 had been a complete success and that the American invasion fleet headed for Taiwan had been driven off with the loss of 25 ships sunk, 12 of them cruisers, battleships, and carriers. In Tokyo this victory was celebrated by dancing in the streets. On October 15 Admiral Toyoda, believing the figures, ordered the Japanese fleet out to pursue the "defeated" enemy.

The fact was that the Halsey raid on Taiwan had been a complete success. The Japanese had lost 179 planes in the air and about 150 on the ground (although the Americans claimed 500 in all). The major airfields of Taiwan were in shambles, runways pockmarked with bomb craters, hangars destroyed, wrecked planes all around. An aircraft arsenal at Takao air base had been reduced to debris. Assessing the results, Admiral Fukudome saw that it was disaster, and as he pored over the reports from Captain Kuno he began to see that they were highly exaggerated.

In Tokyo Imperial General Headquarters was also fooled into believing the tide of war had been turned. But by October 16 Admiral Fukudome had matters in hand again. He had ascertained from reconnaissance planes that the American fleet was intact and steaming away to the Philippines. That day the T Attack Force torpedoed the *Houston* one more time but she survived and was taken into port for repairs. Rear Admiral R. E. Davison's task group hit Luzon on October 15 and 16. The carrier *Franklin* was hit by a bomb, but not seriously damaged. By October 17 it was all over. The Japanese ships that had hurried out of the inland sea to give chase to the "remnants" of the enemy fleet had been informed by Fukudome that the remnants included more than six operating carriers, and so they returned to their base. The two crippled cruisers were on their way to Ulithi, and so were Admiral Halsey's task groups, going in to refuel and rearm and prepare for the invasion of Leyte. Admiral Davison's group fueled and was back in action on October 17, striking Luzon targets. The other task groups followed suit and worked over shipping in Manila Bay and the airfields around Manila. General Kenney's Far Eastern Air Forces, coming from bases on morotai, Biak, and New Guinea, worked over Mindanao airfields and wrecked many planes just being brought in from the Dutch East Indies. The Philippines were encircled by Allied air power. They were being hit in New Guinea, Borneo, the Celebes, the southern Philippines, and the Northern Philippines, and even the Marshalls. B-29s, marine air groups, army air forces, naval land-based air forces, and the carriers were all preparing the way for the Leyte landings, and they produced the greatest disaster to the Japanese air forces that had yet occurred during the war. Rear Admiral Matsuda of the naval air force said after the war that the week before October 20 marked the great change in the air war. Before that time Japan had the air power to respond to any challenge in the normal manner. After that week her air forces were in shreds, and her strategists had to devise new methods of continuing the air war.

CHAPTER NINE

On the Way to Leyte

On October 10 big things began to happen concerning the invasion of the Philippines. On that day a joint army-navy reconnaissance team flew into Leyte in the dark of night in a PBY and landed south of Tacloban. They found the local people and warned them that the invasion was coming and that they should stay away from the beaches.

General MacArthur was in Brisbane preparing for a meeting with General Blamey the Australian commander who would now take over the containment of the bypassed Japanese forces in north and eastern New Guinea. He was getting ready to board the cruiser *Nashville* after the meeting and join the great armada heading for Leyte.

At Manila General Tomoyuki Yamashita was conferring with his staff. He had just arrived the day before from Tokyo after a long exile in Manchuria caused by the personal dislike of General Tōjō, who had shipped him up there immediately after his brilliant campaign in Malaya in 1942. Now, in Japan's hour of need, the army ignored the disgraced Tōjō and turned to this brilliant field commander once again. Yamashita was waiting for the attack he knew was coming and he had already decided on his strategy. He would not sacrifice his men in banzai charges on the beaches, to be mowed down by the fearsome naval and air bombardment the Americans had dealt out in the Gilberts, the Marshalls, and the Marianas. They would defend in depth, and after holding as long as he could in the southern

Philippines he would fight in the mountains of Luzon. It would be a long fight; he had 224,000 men in the Fourteenth Area Army. The defense of the south was entrusted to Lieutenant General Siosaku Suzuki, commander of the Thirty-fifth Army, and it consisted of large garrisons on Mindanao, Cebu, and Leyte islands. The last was defended by Lieutenant General Shiro Makino's Sixteenth Division.

Instructed not to try to fight the Allies on the beaches, General Makino built his defense line in the middle of the Leyte Valley and made the town of Jaro in the central mountains into his supply base. But then he set aside a mobile force that he expected to rush to the beaches and drive the attackers away. They were prepared to participate in the Sho plan, as was the Fourth Air Army, which had about 1,500 aircraft but was suffering from a lack of trained pilots. So great was the need for pilots that the flying schools in Japan were sending them out to the field with even less training than was customary. The army had always believed in training in the field, but those pilots then coming in knew nothing of gunnery or navigation.

The navy had a special problem following the terrible defeat in the battle of the Philippine Sea. After that battle the senior commanders had met to decide what was to be done. All they could do was work with the materials at hand. They had carriers, but the carriers were useless until planes and trained pilots became available for them. They expected another major attack within three or four months after the Saipan invasion and had only surface ships with which to contest it. And to add to that problem, so successful had been the American submarine campaign against shipping around the Japanese homeland, particularly tankers, that the strongest element of the navy, Vice Admiral Takeo Kurita's Second Fleet, had been forced to move from Kure down to Lingga Roads, near Singapore, to be close to the supply of oil for the ships. For air cover the Japanese would have to depend on the army air forces and the shore-based naval air fleets.

That summer at Kure the Japanese battleships and cruisers got radar for the first time. Antiaircraft guns were increased in number and power. In the middle of July Admiral Kurita took his ships to Lingga Roads. Shortly afterward several officers of Kurita's staff flew to Manila for conferences and were informed that naval intelligence there expected the next big Allied push to be headed by General MacArthur and directed at the Philippines. It would come sometime in October, said their informant. Therefore the First Striking Force of the Second Fleet, which included the big battleships *Musashi* and *Yamato*, were to move to Brunei in North Borneo as soon as the coming of the enemy invasion forces could be ascertained, which would have to be by land-based air search. When the landing spot was determined the First Striking Force would move and destroy the enemy transports in the water before they had a chance to land their troops. If for some reason the ships did not arrive in time to stop the landings, they could still destroy the transports, thus crippling the enemy's invasion effort.

For three months at Lingga the Kurita force had trained. They anticipated no combat air patrol to protect them, so they would have to rely on their antiaircraft guns for protection. They practiced ships' evasive maneuvers, ring formation, and mass maneuvering. They practiced for night battles on the theory that they were better night fighters than the Americans. They considered the problems of breaking into the enemy anchorage. They trained and trained. They had the new radar and trained the men in its use. The leaders considered the possibilities of the Allied invasion: Lamon Bay in the north, Leyte Gulf in the middle, and Davao Gulf in the south. Each of these was studied and the passages and geographical information carefully gone over.

Admiral Kurita and his staff opposed the Combined Fleet order that they stay away from the carriers and concentrate on the transports. Kurita felt about the American fleet as Halsey felt about the Japanese—every effort should be made to destroy the American force.

The plan envisaged air cover for the Kurita force from the First and Second Air Fleets operating from the Philippines and Taiwan, but as the Kurita force got ready to move in the second week of October all this had changed completely. The Second Air Fleet had been very hard hit on Taiwan and in the Ryukyus by Admiral Halsey's task force, and the First Air Fleet in the Philippines had never recovered from Halsey's foray in September which had destroyed most of the naval aircraft on Mindanao and in the southern Philippines.

And so Admiral Kurita and his staff waited.

On October 10 the minesweepers and hydrographic ships left Manus for Point Fin, the rendezvous position, off the entrance to Leyte Gulf. Next day the slow LSTs moved out, and on the third day the Dinagat attack group left Hollandia and the bombardment group and the escort carriers left Manus. They would meet on October 17 and begin their work. The battleships and the escort carriers would be on hand from the beginning in case of trouble. General MacArthur concluded his talks with General Blamey and on October 15 flew to Hollandia and conferred with General Kenney and Chief of Staff Sutherland. He also had a brief meeting with President Sergio Osmena of the Philippines, who would be accompanying the invasion forces, although not on MacArthur's ship.

On October 15 the ships of the invasion force first contingent sighted the Palaus. On October 16 General MacArthur boarded the cruiser *Nashville*, which set out to join the invasion forces. Here is the general's recollection of the voyage:

"It is difficult even for one who was there to adquately describe the scene of the next two days. Ships, to the front, to the rear, to the left, and to the right as far as the eye could see their sturdy hulls plowed the water now presenting a broadside view, now their sterns, as they methodically carried out the zigzag tactic of evasion."

By that time the advance force was nearing the Philippines and on October 16 they fueled at sea. Then they headed for

Suluan, Calicoan and Homonhon, three little islands that guard the entrance to Leyte Gulf, where the Japanese could be expected to have watchers. The minesweepers would do their work first, and then the battleships would lay down a barrage and troops would go ashore to eliminate the Japanese.

The minesweeping began at 6:30 on October 17; within 20 minutes the sweepers had been sighted by the Japanese observers and the word was on its way to Combined Fleet Headquarters. The mystery was solved; the invasion would be at Leyte Gulf. Admiral Toyoda was still on Taiwan, and so his staff had to make all the decisions and arrangements. Fortunately the chief of staff knew just what to do. Brunei was alerted, and Admiral Kurita was told to stand by for the move to Leyte. But first the Japanese had to discover the whereabouts of the invasion fleet and their projected time of arrival. Obviously it would be a few days away.

The fire support group moved in and began firing first on Suluan Island. The troops, a company of Rangers, landed and ran to the lighthouse, which they knew was the main observation point of the Japanese. The Japanese had already taken to the jungle, but they were followed and spotted for the Americans by the Filipinos, and one by one they were hunted down and shot.

The next step was to take Dinagat Island, where the Rangers found no Japanese because a guerrilla unit had recently come in and eliminated them. By noon on October 18 the entrance to Leyte Gulf had been secured without much trouble by the Americans. A large number of mines was discovered and the sweeping took a lot of time. On the afternoon of October 18 the underwater demolition teams went into the landing beaches that would take the southern landing force. They found no obstacles, but their boats came under fire from the shore. General Makino's troops were doing the job he had set for them, harassing the landing forces on the beach. Destroyers and cruisers fired on the shore but could not see what they were firing at. The Japanese defenders were well concealed by the overhanging jungle that came to the water's edge. Several landing craft came under fire and in mid-afternoon one of them was sunk. The destroyer *Goldsboroough* was hit by a 75-mm shell, but that was about the only damage done. Two men of the destroyer crew were killed.

On October 19 the Americans suffered their first ship casualty. The destroyer *Ross* hit a mine off Homonhon Island, then hit another before she stopped and began to list. The tug *Chickasaw* picked her up, but the destroyer was out of the fight. She lost 23 men killed and nine wounded, but she survived.

At daylight on this day before the invasion the Japanese began firing on the underwater demolition teams off Tacloban. The destroyers moved in close and came under fire from shore guns. But the work continued, getting ready for the next day's landings.

That day the 12 escort carriers performed their missions to support the landings by hitting enemy airfields and targets on the land. Admiral Halsey had been delayed by the damage to his two cruisers in the Taiwan operation, so the responsibility for air defense rested with the escorts and their commander, Rear Admiral Thomas L. Sprague. For three days, from October 18 to October 20, the escort carriers bore the full responsibility for air support of the growing armada that appeared at the ends of Leyte Gulf. They did a fine job, apparently to the surprise of the high command of the Seventh Fleet, who did not seem to have as much confidence in the small carriers as they should have had, a sign of the tendency of the military men to underrate new weapons.

The escort carrier planes struck the enemy defenses and transportation on Leyte; hit aircraft and installations on the airfields of Cebu, Negros, Panay, and Mindanao; and attacked shipping when they saw it in the shore waters. The small carriers put up nearly 500 sorties, about half of them against Leyte and the other half against the nearby island airfields.

A fighter from the carrier *Chenango* was shot down over Opon Field on Cebu but the pilot managed to make a water landing and was rescued by Filipinos who were eager to help further the invasion. By noon on October 18 all the little islands were secure. A few Japanese aircraft attacked, but halfheartedly.

On October 19 the carrier planes continued to work over the island area, but they did not seem to find much opposition. The fact was that the Japanese air forces had received so many blows recently that they were virtually moribund. One or two fighters would be seen occasionally, but they would disappear before they could be reached. Some planes were destroyed on the ground, but it was suspected that many of them were plants, fake planes put down by the Japanese to draw fire.

Admiral Oldendorf's bombardment force of cruisers, old battleships, and destroyers was very active on October 19, bombarding southern Leyte to soften it up for the landings the next day.

Rear Admiral G. L. Weyler's Northern Bombardment Group, which was to cover the Tacloban area, began working on October 19, too. The battleship *Mississippi* went into action at about 9 o'clock in the morning and soon claimed to have blown up a Japanese ammunition dump. By mid-afternoon she had started fires in several areas. The destroyer *Aulick* spent much of the day close inshore, and her crew received a lesson to remind them that the Japanese were still very much in the war. The *Aulick* was standing at about 2,800 yards out to cover the underwater demolition teams and opened fire, with her 40-mm guns and five- inch guns on a group of huts that seemed to hide machine guns. Just before noon the Japanese made a hit with a shore gun on a landing craft, which promptly sank. Then the *Aulick* came under fire from machine guns and three-inch shore guns coming from two sides, White Beach and a little island offshore. The Japanese fired quickly and accurately and made several direct hits on the destroyer, killing two men, wounding 12, and hitting the guns so that two of them had to revert to manual fire control.

The main body of the invasion force began to appear off Point Fin at about 11 P.M. on October 19. Admiral Wilkinson led what he called "the parade," which would end in the landing of the troops, scheduled by both northern and southern landing groups for 10 o'clock on the morning of October 20.

General MacArthur recalled the time:

We came to Leyte just before midnight of a dark and moonless night. The stygian waters below and the black sky above seemed to conspire in wrapping us in an invisible cloak as we lay to and waited for dawn before entering Leyte Gulf. Phase one of the plan had been accomplished with little resistance. Now and then a ghostly ship would slide quietly by us, looming out of the night and disappearing into the gloom almost before its outline could be depicted. I knew that on every ship nervous men lined the rails or paced the decks, peering into the darkness and wondering what stood out there beyond the night waiting for the dawn to come. There is a universal sameness in the emotions of men whether they be admiral or sailor, general or private, at such a time as this. On almost every ship one could count on seeing groups huddled around maps in the wardrooms, infantrymen nervously inspecting their rifles, the crews of the ships testing their gear, last minute letters being written, men with special missions or objectives trying to visualize them again. For every man there were tons of supplies, and equipment,—trucks and vehicles of all kinds and more than one ton of ammunition for every man who would storm those shores. Late that evening I went back to my cabin and read again those passages from the Bible from which I have always gained inspiration and hope. And I prayed that a merciful God would preserve each one of those men on the morrow.

CHAPTER TEN

Landing at Leyte

Early on the morning of October 20, 1944, planes from the Task Force 38 carriers *Wasp, Hornet, Monterey, Cowpens, Franklin, Enterprise, San Jacinto*, and *Belleau Wood* ranged over the beaches and the towns and the airfields, firing machine guns and bombing anything that seemed to be Japanese. At about 7 A.M. the battleships *Mississippi, Maryland*, and *West Virginia* approached the northern landing area and began firing on the beach. After they had fired 30 shells per gun they moved off and Admiral Berkey's ships came in to replace them. They were the cruisers *Phoenix, Boise, Australia*, and *Shropshire*, representing American and Australian navies. Also fire support destroyers were brought in to give help to the landing troops when they needed it.

General MacArthur, aboard the *Nashville*, was awakened by the sound of the barrage. He arose, dressed, picked up a revolver, and slipped it into his trousers pocket just as General Courtney Whitney of his staff entered the cabin. That revolver, MacArthur said, with a touch of the actor, had belonged to his father, General Arthur MacArthur, who had carried it in the hard days of the Philippine Rebellion. He was taking it along just in case, because he had said many times in the past that the Japanese would never take him alive. This sort of exaggeration was completely natural to MacArthur, who seemed always to live in a sort of dream world of his own building. But as always the MacArthur theatricality touched a chord with the American people who needed heroes. And quite naturally everything MacArthur did seemed larger than life. It was only his peers in the military establishment who found him hard to bear.

MacArthur then went up to the captain's bridge of the *Nashville* and joined the crowd of officers and war correspondents gathered there. He was wearing his gold braid cap and his sunglasses, and he had his old corncob pipe clutched in his teeth. The photographers snapped away as the general looked out at the beach. There was Tacloban ahead, the site of one of his first military assignments. As a young second lieutenenat just freshly graduated from the U.S. Military Academy, MacArthur had been assigned to make a survey of Tacloban's possibilities as a base in time of war. Now he was seeing the base from the other end of the stick. A war correspondent asked the general how he thought the battle was going, and without looking up from the beach MacArthur said it was going just fine. Then he added that it was the Sixteenth Japanese division that they were fighting that day—the division that had been involved in the Bataan Death March.

The air cover seemed to disappear with the naval bombardment, and there was a reason. Admiral Barbey had ordered the planes to stay clear for 45 minutes before H-Hour. So from 9:15 to 10 o'clock the planes stayed away from the beach, but they were out and up there, hitting airfields and other targets. Admiral Sherman's carriers, the *Essex, Lexington, Princeton* and *Langley*, and Admiral Bogan's *Intrepid, Hancock, Bunker Hill, Cabot* and *Independence* were all conducting day patrols, and the escort carriers kept 16 fighters and six torpedo bombers in the air all that day.

By 9:30 the transports had their boats in the water and the boat waves had formed up. They took off for the shore at 9:43, preceded by 11 landing craft fitted with rocket launchers to plaster the beach ahead. Soon 5,500 four and-a-half-inch rockets were crashing onto Beach Red and Beach White. At this point the covering ships lifted their fire and began seeking targets inland. The Japanese were firing back with mortars and guns in the hills behind the beach.

And so the landings began, historic landings really, although the GIs involved were more interested in keeping their heads down and not getting shot than in the historic significance of the occasion. The history would be for later reading; just then they were busy fighting. But the history was there. Only 30 months earlier General MacArthur had been summoned to Australia and thus saved from the fate of the men of the Philippines. He had been given a half million dollars by the government of the Philippines, a Medal of Honor by Congress (which he certainly deserved only symbolically), and a command that was much less meaningful than it seemed. But he had persevered and had won the political ear of President Roosevelt for his perseverance in insisting that return to the Philippines was an essential factor in American policy. And here he was coming "home" again, proving to the people of Asia that the Americans lived up to their promises. This was the political signficance of the Leyte landings, but it was far beyond the interest of the soldiers and sailors involved. Their war was never politically motivated; the American military and political machinery had never seen this as necessary. Americans fought for mom and apple pie, but they also fought because they believed their leaders and left the decisions to them, just wanting to get the misery over with.

The landings of Admiral Barbey's group on Beach Red were not so very easy. To be sure this amphibious operation was a good one, with no surf to worry the men, good weather, and no mines or underwater obstacles. The Japanese mortar fire from the hills was disconcertaing and dangerous. Two LCVPs from the transport *Elmore* were hit and a boat from the *Aquarius* was sunk in the first few waves. The LSTs had to come to the beach to land their cargoes and came under fire at 10:45 when they approached Beach Red. In the first five minutes three of them were hit and one,

LST-181, was set afire. There were about 50 casualties.

The mortaring stopped then for a time but resumed again around noon and LST-181 was hit again and lost her power. She had 36 casualties and her cargo was lost. Another LST ran aground, and there was a good deal of confusion in the LST fleet.

The Seventh Cavalry landed on Beach Red and then pushed forward to a small airstrip that was its first objective. The troops of the Twenty-fourth Division raced ashore and planted American and Filipino flags symbolically on the beach.

Rear Admiral W. M. Fechteler's *San Ricardo* landing went much more smoothly. Beach White had no problems; the landings were almost unopposed. One enemy gun fired at the landing troops but the destroyer *Boise* began shooting and the firing stopped. By mid- afternoon the unloading was proceeding steadily.

Down south, on beaches Violet and Yellow, the troops of the Twenty-fourth Corps were also going ashore, near Dulag. The only opposition came from mortar fire, which killed and wounded several men. But when the soldiers looked for some way to retaliate, they could find nothing to shoot at.

The Ninety-sixth Division moved rapidly, and an hour after landing they captured their objective, Hill 120. The Seventh Division had a mixed greeting from the Japanese. The 184th Regiment was almost unopposed and seized Dulag airfield, but the 232nd Infantry ran into stubborn opposition from machine guns and had to bring up tanks to clear the area. After firing for a while General Suzuki's men fell back to the hills.

On the Tacloban beach, the first wave hit opposition; the second wave hit less. Shortly after noon it was time for the third wave. General MacArthur, who had eaten an early lunch and changed into a fresh uniform, appeared on the bridge of the *Nashville*. He was going in with this wave now that it seemed relatively safe. "Relatively" was the operative word, because with the Japanese, experience had proved that almost anything could happen.

The time came. He clambered down a ladder and into a boat. The coxswain took the boat to the transport *John Land* to pick up Philippine President Sergio Osmena, who had succeeded Manuel Quezon after his death, and Carlos P. Romulo, a budding political leader. Then the boat headed for the shore, now full of MacArthurs' staff and war correspondents, with other boats trailing behind.

General MacArthur sat like a ramrod in the stern of his landing craft, and when it grounded suddenly about 50 yards offshore, he told the coxswain to lower the ramp and then with an aside to General Sutherland, who had escaped with him from Corregidor 30 months before, he walked down the ramp and began wading to the shore in water knee-deep. When he reached the beach, apparently oblivious to the possibility of snipers in the trees, he walked to a little mound and stood on it, stopped, and lit up his corncob pipe.

The landings went on around him. In the distance could be heard the high-pitched rattle of a Japanese machine gun. Then heavy firing broke out inland, and MacArthur strolled in that direction. He came across a squad of Twenty-fourth Division infantrymen and asked how they found the enemy. He saw some dead Japanese and turned over the bodies with his foot to examine their insignia, and verified that they were indeed the Sixteenth Division, which had been on Bataan.

Not far away signalmen were setting up a portable broadcasting unit. It had been arranged that MacArthur would make a broadcast from that spot on that day, symbolizing America's return to the Philippines. The broadcast would be aired in America and in the Philippines as well. He took up the microphone.

"This is the Voice of Freedom," he began. Those were symbolic words. The last broadcasts from Corregidor under siege by the Japanese had begun with that opening, and after the fall of Corregidor the voice had been still for many months. Now it had returned.

People of the Philippines. I have returned. By the grace of Almighty God our forces stand again on Philippine soil—soil consecrated in the blood of our two peoples.

At my side is your President, Sergio Osmena, worthy successor to that great patriot Manuel Quezon, with members of his cabinet. The seat of your government is therefore now firmly established on Philippine soil. Rally to me. Let the indomitable spirit of Bataan and Corregidor lead on.

As the lines of battle roll forward to bring you within the zone of operations, rise and strike. For your homes and hearths, strike! In the name of your sacred dead, strike!

Let no heart be faint. Let every arm be steeled. The guidance of Divine God points the way. Follow in his name to the Holy Grail of righteous victory.

After the speech, MacArthur and Osmena walked inland for a way and then sat down on a fallen log and talked. Around them the sights and sounds of the invasion continued, a Japanese plane flew over the area and dropped two bombs, machine guns and rifles rattled their fire. After their talk MacArthur and Osmena got into a jeep and were driven to the front line, where the Seventh Cavalry was assaulting Tacloban airfield. Expressing himself as extremely satisfied with the progress of the invasion, MacArthur then returned to the *Nashville*. The invasion went on. He made more broadcasts, one to the guerrillas who had been operating behind Japanese lines since 1941.

"To my leaders behind enemy lines. The campaign of occupation has commenced. It is desired that your forces be committed to action with the specific mission of harassing the movement of enemy troops."

General MacArthur witnessed the northern landings, but he learned about the southern landings from his staff. They were carried out 11 miles south of Beach Red. The drill was the same: aerial support early in the morning, then the naval bombardment that reached its apogee at about 9:30, and the departure of the landing craft from the line of ships, with their churning wakes. The first wave hit the beach just before 10 o'clock, almost perfectly on schedule. The ships shifted their gunfire a mile inland. One particular point of aim was Cannon Hill, a 1,000-foot eminence a little way inland that was presumed to be crawling with Japanese. The assumption was proved out when a 75-mm battery straddled the destroyer *Bennion* several times and wounded several men with a near-miss.

Dulag was captured by the Seventh Division troops at about noon. The Ninety-sixth Division landing on Beach Blue did not run into resistance until it reached the base of Hill 120, about 25 minutes after landing. The hill was taken by the 382nd Infantry and the American flag raised atop it at 10:42. By noon most of the troops of Twenty-fourth Corps were ashore. The ships moved in closer and the unloading began on Beach Yellow. Operations had to be held up during part of the afternoon because of concentrated mortar fire, but landing craft equipped with mortars were sent to rout out those enemy troops and did by the end of the afternoon.

The day had been surprisingly easy in both landing areas, with so little air opposition as to seem negligable. But in late afternoon came an incident that indicated something of the future off the Leyte shore.

The light cruiser *Honolulu*, the flagship of Rear Admiral Walden L. Ainsworth, had been assigned to bombardment duty in the southern landings. That job was completed by noon and the *Honolulu* stood by in the gulf, about five miles offshore, ready to fire on any targets the army called for. Her captain was in his sea cabion near the bridge having his hair cut when a lookout sang out:

"Torpedo plane port quarter."

The captain leaped to the bridge just in time to see the Japanese plane approach the *Honolulu* from out of the overcast and drop a torpedo. He saw the wake, ordered full speed astern, but could not get out of the way of the torpedo, which struck the ship forward of the bridge on the port side, tearing a hole in her 25 feet by 29 feet and killing 60 officers and men, and doing much damage to the vessel. She went dead in the water. She was saved that day and her wounded were taken off by a destroyer. But the invasion had claimed its first major ship casualty.

The fact that there was so little aerial activity came as a surprise to the invaders. But the reason for it was simple enough. The Japanese naval air force was in disarray and the army air force was not yet ready to cooperate in the battle. This particular attack had come from the 331st Air Group of the First Air Fleet, which had been given the assignment of stopping the American invasion of Leyte. The assignment was obviously impossible. The 331st that day could put in the air only two torpedo bombers.

Here is the unit's operation report:

"Tenzan attack plane took off Nichols No. 1 at 12320 and another Tenzan took off at 1400 for attack on enemy ships in Leyte Gulf. Sighted enemy 1600 (8 battleships, 20 cruisers, 30 destroyers, 30 transports) and immediately went in for attack. Torpedo released from altitude of 10 meters. One large transport definitely sunk. Attack completed 1620. One plane landed at Cebu Base, 1705. Second plane failed to return."

This had to be the attack on the *Honolulu* despite the misidentification of the ship, for she was the only vessel torpedoed that first day.

But much more would· be happening soon, because the Japanese were just now planning Draconian measures to make up for their extreme shortage of aircraft in the Philippines.

In conjunction with the Sho Operation, when Admiral Toyoda had visited Manila a few days earlier he had decided to make a change in the air command of the First Air Fleet, which was then under Vice Admiral Kimpei Teraoka. Admiral Teraoka was a competent commander, but he did not believe in sacrificing his people and therefore did not seem to be as aggressive as Admiral Toyada thought he should be. He would be brought back to Japan and put in charge of a training program where his great experience would serve well and his lack of aggression would not hurt the war effort.

Admiral Takejiro Ohnishi had arrived in Manila on October 17 to be greeted with the news that the invaders were on their way and had moved to the edge of Leyte Gulf. He knew that he was expected to support the Sho Operation with everything he had. But looking around he was appalled to find that he had virtually nothing with which to work—the First Air Fleet had been decimated by Admiral Halsey's attacks and could put fewer than a hundred planes into the air.

Because of this Ohnishi decided that he would have to begin a drastic program, making every air attack count to the utmost. This required that his pilots sacrifice themselves by diving their aircraft into enemy ships, preferably aircraft carriers. On October 19 Admiral Ohnishi laid this plan out for his staff and then went to the fighter field at Mabalacat to try the plan on one of his best air groups, the 201st Air Group, which had a distinguished record. He had gone to Mabalacat, talked to the young men there about the gravity of the situation facing Japan, and accepted their vows that there was nothing they would like better than to commit suicide in behalf of emperor and country. That very night they had organized the Shimpu Special Attack Corps, consisting of 24 young men, each eager to die for Japan. That very night they also learned of the appearance of Halsey's carriers 60 miles east of Suluan Island. They were ready to launch their first suicide mission when a force of American planes appeared over the field and destroyed all the aircraft on the runways. But the idea was born, and that night mechanics began assembling planes from parts of destroyed aircraft. The idea had taken a powerful grip on the minds of the young men of the 201st Air Group and it would not die.

By the end of invasion day about 80,000 troops were ashore. The Tenth Corps troops around Tacloban had secured the San Juanico Strait between Leyte and Samar, and by mid-afternoon had cleared the Cataisan Peninsula of all enemy troops. The Twenty-fourth Division, after some hard fighting, had taken Mount Guinhandang. By 6 P.M. the Northern Force transports had completed their unloading and were ready to leave the area.

The Southern Attack Force controlled the coast of Leyte Island from the north bank of the Libernan River to the mouth of the Marabang River. The Seventh Division had advanced farther than expected, although the Ninety-sixth had been held up by a difficult swamp. Major General John Hodge was ashore and ready to carry on the land campaign.

There was one dangerous aspect to the invasion that did not at the moment appear too serious. Because of the mortaring of the LSTs and the damage to several of them, many were diverted that day to the Tacloban airstrip area and it became in reality a supply dump. In a few days the beaches there would be filled with ammunition, food, and gasoline, piled high, and the army commands would be camped very near these dumps. "Just two cruisers loose in that gulf could have cleaned up an awful lot," Admiral Kinkaid said. If the enemy ships had destroyed those at any time after a day the invasion could have been delayed indefinitely.

And just such an incursion was what the Japanese high command was planning and had already set in motion.

CHAPTER ELEVEN

The Japanese Move

On October 21, the day after the Leyte landings, the portent of things to come arrived off the Tacloban beachhead when just after first light, a Japanese plane crashed into the foremast of the HMAS *Australia*. The pilot may have erred in his attack or he may have decided to commit suicide in hopes of sinking an Allied ship. It must have been an army plane because there was no note of any navy operations at that hour. The damage to the *Australia* was considerable; the captain of the ship was killed, along with 19 men, and the senior Australian officer who was aboard and 53 men were wounded.

That day General MacArthur went ashore again and toured around the edge of the battle. The First Cavalry Division was fighting along the trails and on the airfields. MacArthur was impatient for the moment that General Kenney could make the airfield operational. He wanted to get ashore. Admiral Kinkaid also was anxious for General MacArthur to go ashore because he wanted the *Nashville* as a fighting ship, not a hotel for generals. But it was going to take a little time.

At 3 P.M. on October 21 the Japanese suicide squad at Mabalacat airfield was alerted. A report had come in about six carriers east of Suluan Island. The operations office went to work and got three Zeros ready to go out and attack the enemy. But then an American air raid destroyed all three planes. Three more planes were readied and took off on the first suicide missions. But two came back and there was no record of any suicide plane hitting an American ship on that afternoon of October 21.

One of the major problems of the Japanese naval forces was the shortage of search planes. They were finding it most difficult to discover the American ships because their regular search elements had been so badly decimated by the Halsey raids of September. Now Admiral Fukudome's scene of operations was shifted to the Philippines and he began the movement of his 350 aircraft. From Imperial Headquarters came word that the Sho Operation's three-pronged naval attack would arrive on the morning of October 25, and so the major air effort should begin the day before to soften up the American defenses. Fukudome was planning for a conventional attack of 250 planes on October 24.

On October 22, having new orders from Imperial General Headquarters, Field Marshal Hisaichi Terauchi, the commander of the Japanese Southern Armies, ordered General Yamashita to change his plan for the defense of the Philippines. Yamashita, after his arrival, had reported to Terauchi, who had moved his headquarters of the southern forces from Singapore to Manila. He had explained his plan of fighting the major battle on Luzon, and Terauchi had concurred. But now that all was to be changed. After several sessions, Terauchi said that Yamashita must muster all possible strength to destroy the enemy at Leyte, in connection with the Sho Operation.

Hearing of the arrival of Admiral Fukudome's Second Air Fleet, funneling in army planes for the coming battle, and knowing of the movements of the naval forces toward Leyte, Terauchi and his staff on the night of October 22 were ebullient about the coming battle and the victory they expected. Someone on the staff suggested that they demand the surrender of the entire American army just as soon as they captured General MacArthur!

Admiral Ohnishi found it hard to contemplate the present at all. His First Air Fleet virtually did not exist on the operational level. He had established four suicide units, the Shikishima, Asahi, Yamazukura, and Yamato. Three were located at Mabalacat on Luzon and the fourth at the southern island of Cebu. They had a total of 13 aircraft. Of course, coming from Japan, Admiral Ohnishi was aware of the production of the Japanese aircraft industry, which was increasing at this time in spite of all the problems with supplies. But building planes in Japan and getting them to the Philippines were two separate problems. Admiral Ohnishi needed aircraft and he needed them *now*—as soon as they could be brought to the Philippines. Unlike other elements of the Japanese air forces, at the moment he had no shortage of pilots. He had too many pilots clamoring for planes.

The battle on Leyte was going very well for the invading Americans. The escort carriers were doing their job of troop support magnificently, keeping an air umbrella over the beaches and hitting targets inland, concentrating on airfields. The Japanese were now adept at concealment of aircraft, sometimes keeping them a mile from the airfield and pushing them under cover of darkness in small groups. There was no more of the carelessness exhibited in New Guinea in April, when the Japanese had been so confident of their air strength in the Hollandia area that they had kept their aircraft lined up for quick action on the aprons and runways of the three airfields. They had been confident that the Allies could not reach them from the Australian and southern New Guinea airfields. This surmise had been correct until the winter of 1944 when the P-38 Lightning had been modified with extra gas tanks to give them much more range. In four raids in April General Kenney's aircraft had destroyed 400 planes, most of them on the ground. Now the Japanese never left operational aircraft unprotected on the airfields during daylight hours.

After the Kurita force sailed, it headed up to cross toward the Palawan Passage that runs alongside the snakelike Puerta Princessa Island on the outside eastern edge of the Philippine archipelago. There they encountered the American submarines *Darter* and *Dace*, which were patrolling the area. They had sunk two freighters from a Japanese convoy on October 12, but had been patrolling fruitlessly since that time.

The dry period suddenly ended for the two submarines at 1 o'clock on the morning of October 23 when Commander David McClintock's radar operator reported blips on his screen 17 miles away. The two submarines were on the surface and McClintock shouted to Commander Balden D. Claggett of the *Dace* that they had something. They were off the southern entrance to Palawan Passage and the Kurita force—29 ships—was coming up in a nice neat formation of five lines. The Americans did not see all the ships, but they saw enough big ships to realize that the Japanese had a major force at sea, heading up the Palawan passage, obviously bound for the Philippines. They radioed Admiral Ralph Christie in Australia, who informed Admiral Halsey, so that the Third Fleet could begin looking for the Japanese, and then the submarines began the hunt.

They were traveling on the surface at 19 knots and the Kurita force was moving at 16 knots. At 5:25 that morning the *Darter* was about 11 miles away, with the Japanese ships heading directly toward the submarine. It was the custom of Japanese fleet units to keep an air antisubmarine patrol out in front, but because of the fuel shortage this protection had been denied Admiral Kurita. All the seaplanes carried by the big ships had been transferred ashore recently because of the submarine threat that made it impossible for a ship to stop and recover its planes.

Just after 6 A.M. on October 23 Commander McClintock's *Darter* submerged and so did the *Dace*, not far away. At 6:30 *Darter* was only half a mile from the leading ship, the cruiser *Atago*, which was Admiral Kurita's flagship. McClintock fired six torpedoes at the ship and then swung around to fire four torpedoes at the second ship in the line, the cruiser *Takao*. When McClintock raised the periscope he could see that the *Atago* was a mass of flame and smoke and was already sinking by the bow. The *Takao* was floundering;

the two torpedoes that hit her blew off the rudder and two propellers and flooded three boiler rooms.

Before the *Atago* went down, Admiral Kurita and his staff were ready to be transferred to the destroyer *Kishinami*, but the ship sank beneath them and they had swim for it. Later they moved to the battleship *Yamato*.

While the *Darter* was sinking the *Atago* and damaging the *Takao* so severely that she had to head back to Brunei Bay, the *Dace* was firing four torpedoes into the heavy cruiser *Maya*, which exploded and sank immediately.

After that Vice Admiral Matome Ugaki in the *Yamato* assumed temporary control of the fleet and put the speed up to 24 knots so they could get away from the submarines.

Later in the day the two submarines surfaced and the commanders talked about making another attack on the crippled *Takao*, but when they detected radar, they decided against it as too dangerous under the circumstances—too many destroyers about. That was not the only danger as it turned out. The sea on the eastern side of Palawan Passage was full of shallows, and that night the *Darter* ran aground on a rock. The crew did all they could to get the submarine afloat but it was impossible. They had to be rescued by the *Dace*, and the crowded *Dace* headed for Perth.

It was mid-afternoon on October 23 before Admiral Kurita and his staff boarded the *Yamato* and the admiral again took command of the fighting force. They steamed ahead, toward San Bernardino Strait, but first through the Sibuyan Sea.

On October 23 the Americans knew the Japanese were going to make some sort of naval effort to stop the Leyte invasion. They had the news of the torpedoing of the *Atago* and the *Takao*, and of the Japanese cruiser *Aoba* by the submarine *Bream*, off Luzon. They also had the report that the Japanese force was continuing on. Actually there were four major forces moving toward Leyte but the Americans then knew about only two of them, the Kurita force and the ships of Rear Admiral Hiyokide Shima, three cruisers and four destroyers that were suppose to join Admiral Nishimura at Surigao Strait. Just now on October 23 Shima was about to enter Coron Bay where a tanker was supposed to be waiting to fuel his ships for the dash to Surigao.

Far away, off Taiwan, Admiral Ozawa that day was moving toward the Philippines too. His captains were worried about the submarine threat and kept a constant submarine patrol in the air. On the morning of October 23 the battleship-carrier *Izuzu* reported a submarine. It was the fourth or fifth time that a submarine alert had been called in the last few days, but the crews dutifully went to general quarters. Again the submarine threat was illusory, but later that day Admiral Ozawa's radio men picked up transmissions of the Halsey fleet, and they were so clear that the admiral soon knew that the Americans were close by. The frustrating thing was that it was Ozawa's responsibility to be found by the Americans, who thus would be diverted from the Kurita and Nishimura forces, but the Americans stubbornly refused to send planes to a point where they could spot Ozawa.

One reason for that was the preoccupation of Admiral Halsey's airmen with the Kurita force. Admiral Bogan's task group was fueling that day, but Halsey ordered Bogan to make searches on the morning of October 23 in and around Coron Bay (where Admiral Shima was fueling). At the moment Halsey was using Admiral Sherman's task group to make air strikes on Luzon and Lingayen Gulf, looking for aircraft and ships and finding some. But somewhere out there were two major Japanese naval units—maybe more—and the search planes had not found them. Another interesting fact reported to Kinkaid by his escort carriers was that the Japanese were funneling a lot of aircraft into the Philippines at that moment. At noon on October 23 escort carrier planes had hit fields in the Visayas and on Mindanao, all fields that had been thoroughly worked over many times in the recent past, and they reported many aircraft, some of which they had destroyed.

Ashore on Leyte the Tenth Corps had taken army control of the landings on October 22 and General Hodge had taken control of the Twenty-fourth Corps on October 23. West of

Dulag the Twenty-fourth Corps was running into difficulty from more serious Japanese opposition, and in the hills beyond Tacloban the Tenth Corps was also finding the resistance stiffening. That day President Osmena, General MacArthur, and all the senior officers of the operation assembled at Tacloban for a ceremonial reestablishment of the government of the Philippine Commonwealth on Filipino soil. Photos were taken of the outside of the provincial capital building, which looked just fine, but inside the building was a complete shambles. For the guard of honor the officers rounded up two troops of dirty, tired soldiers of the First Cavalry. A microphone was set up on the steps and the ceremony was broadcast throughout the Philippines. A bugler sounded colors and the American and Philippines flags were hoisted simultaneously. General MacArthur then presented the Distinguished Service Cross to Kangleon, a guerrilla leader who had been appointed acting governor of Leyte. For some reason no one had notified the people of Tacloban, so few of them attended. But the word got out and by the time the ceremony broke up Filipinos were coming to town to line the street and cheer the Americans.

In Tacloban that day, General MacArthur visited the Walter Price house, which his staff had suggested would do for his quarters and the offices of general headquarters. It was located in the center of Tacloban, three blocks from the provincial capital which President Osmena would use until he could return to Manila.

MacArthur said the Price house would do just fine, and so the work started to make it usable as residence and staff office. As this was going on, so were the Japanese air raids, which increased remarkably in intensity on the 23rd, as Admiral Fukudome prepared for the big raid of the next day and brought in more planes. The situation ashore was worrisome to Admiral Kinkaid, who knew how little interference it would take to make a shambles of his beaches, now chockablock with gasoline, ammunition, and other supplies for the troops.

In the Philippines, the Japanese air forces were furiously funneling in planes as the escort carrier pilots had noticed. The Second Air Fleet had brought in nearly 200 planes. The army air force had brought in more. But because of the continued American air attacks, many installations were hard put to handle the influx, and when one whole group of aircraft arrived at Clark Field there were too many to be landed, and so they were diverted to other fields. It took several days to round them up and get them into one place.

On that night of October 23, Admiral Ozawa ordered his radio men to break radio silence and send a long radio message from the flagship *Zuikaku*, expecting the Americans to pick it up and giving them plenty of time to do so. But the American radio monitors were otherwise engaged and paid no attention to the message. Ozawa, whose job it was to attract Halsey's attention, was disappointed and decided to change course and head southwest. At that point he was about 200 miles north of Luzon, but no one was looking that way.

Admiral Halsey's attention was focused on reports of the sighting of three different forces: Admiral Kurita's center force on the north in the Sibuyan Sea, and Admiral Nishimura and Admiral Shima heading for Surigao Strait. By the afternoon of October 23 both Admiral Halsey and Admiral Kinkaid were anticipating battle with the Japanese naval forces. At noon Admiral Bogan's task group and Admiral Davison's task group were operating northeast of Samar. Bogan moved in close to San Bernardino Strait, and Davison moved south near Leyte Gulf. Admiral John McCain's group had been sent to Ulithi for food, fuel, and ammunition, but it was now pulled back to launch dawn searches for the enemy. Admiral Sherman's group was east of the Polillo Islands. covering the west coast of Luzon.

On the night of October 23 Admiral Fukudome ordered long-range flying boats to make a comprehensive night search of the waters around the Philippines. He was in search of Admiral Halsey's Third Fleet, too, and he already had plans for a massive attack as soon as it was found. The pilots of the Second Air Fleet had orders to man their planes at dawn.

At a few minutes after midnight one of the flying boats sighted a large force offshore 250 miles from Manila, and when Admiral Fukudome was told he decided to launch a predawn attack. The weather was terrible, as was quite common in late October, but there was nothing to be done about that. If the planes could fly, they would.

The planes took off in the darkness from Clark Field and its satellites. They moved out in two waves and headed due east from Manila. But the weather was so bad that they found nothing at the 250-mile mark or anywhere near it. One bomber pilot caught sight of a ship down below, but he could not identify it and when he went down he could not find it again. So the two waves of attackers turned around and went back to base.

At daybreak the three American carrier groups in the east launched search teams to look around the west coast of Luzon and the Sibuyan, Sulu, and Mindanao seas for enemy ships.

At 6:30 in the morning the weather had not improved much; it was a squally overcast day everywhere around the islands, but the visibilty had increased with the coming of daylight and the Japanese tried again. This time they found three of Admiral Halsey's task groups off the eastern shore of the islands, 150 to 200 miles out.

Almost simultaneously one of Admiral Halsey's search planes sighted the battleship *Yamato*, which was just rounding the southern tip of Mindoro Island and entering Tablas Strait.

The Japanese attacked. A group of 60 aircraft came down out of the clouds to strike Admiral Sherman's task group. Seven fighters were scrambled from the carier *Essex*, led by David McCampbell, the *Essex* air group commander. At 8:33 McCampbell fired his first shot at a group of fighters and bombers. The bombers broke away and the fighters went into an aerial maneuver known as the

Lufbery circle, but McCampbell and his wingman, Lieutenant (jg) R. W. Rushing, maintained altitude and waited until the fighters came out of the circle, as did the other planes of the squadron. In the next hour they shot down at least 25 Japanese aircraft. Other air groups had similar experiences, but the enemy also scored that day. The destroyer *Leutze* was damaged, the oiler *Ashtabula* was hit, and the *LST 552* was also damaged. But the biggest shock of the day was the attack on Admiral Sherman's task group.

A single plane that had been hiding above the overcast, while dozens were shot down, came screaming down and dropped a single 550-pound bomb on the flight deck of the carrier *Princeton*. The bomb passed through three decks and the blast entered the hangar deck where it set fire to six torpedo bomber TBFs that had been taken below, and soon their torpedoes were exploding. These explosions wrecked the forward and after elevators. Soon the ship was in dire peril and all but the firefighters evacuated. The cruiser *Birmingham* aided in the rescue as did the destroyers *Gatling, Irwin, Cassin Young*, and *Morrison*. For a while it seemed that the fires could be put out, but a fire reached the torpedo stowage area, and the explosion of torpedoes blew off most of the ship's stern. Then it was obvious that the *Princeton* could not be saved and the destroyer *Irwin* tried to torpedo her. The first torpedo exploded on the ship's bow but did not do much damage. The second missed, the third porpoised and very nearly came back to torpedo the *Irwin*. Torpedo four missed and so did torpedo five. Number six again nearly came back to hit *Irwin*. At that point the *Irwin* was relieved of the responsibility and the cruiser *Reno* fired two torpedoes. The first one hit the *Princeton* and blew the ship to pieces, creating a big mushroom cloud over the wreckage as the gasoline storage (100,000 gallons) exploded.

The Japanese account of the air battle against the American carriers that day is terse and not very informative except as to the death of the *Princeton*:

The first and second waves of attack planes converged upon the first group of surface craft and made a direct hit with 250 kg bombs on a large regular carrier. They set fire to one battleship, set fire and inflicted considerable damage on a cruiser, and shot down at least 32 enemy planes. Our losses were 67 planes missing. The third attack (three carrier bombers) took off in the afternoon but returned owing to bad weather. Following this, 24 planes in three groups took to the air in search of the enemy's third group with carriers . . .

But while the fighters of the American fleet were fending off the Japanese and shooting them down in wholesale lots, and the seamen in Admiral Sherman's task group were trying to save the *Princeton*, the task force bombers were heading in to the Sibuyan Sea to attack Admiral Kurita's force.

The first strike to reach Kurita was launched by the carriers *Cabot* and *Intrepid* just after 9 o'clock that morning of October 24. They found the antiaircraft fire intense, but no combat air patrol over the Japanese ships. So the battle of planes against ships began, the second battle of its sort in history,* and one that once and for all—had there been the shadow a doubt left—established the Billy Mitchell theory that with no other factors intervening, airplanes could sink battleships.

*The first battle of aircraft against battleships was the sinking of the British battle cruiser *Repulse* and the new battleship *Prince of Wales* by Japanese land-based aircraft in the opening days of the Pacific war.

CHAPTER TWELVE

The Battle of the Sibuyan Sea

On the morning of October 24 as his ships headed through the Sibuyan Sea Admiral Kurita knew that he was going to be running a gauntlet in a few hours, and that he would have to protect himself. He had sent messages to Manila asking for fighter protection, and the messages had gone unanswered. There were reasons, and they were simple enough: Admiral Fukudome's Second Air Fleet was preoccupied with the strikes against the American carriers, and Admiral Ohnishi did not have any planes to send. The only planes that could have been sent to Kurita's aid were army planes, and the liaison between naval and army forces was nonexistent at this level, no matter what the admirals and generals said in Tokyo.

Kurita's first warning of what was in the offing came to him that morning when Manila radioed the news of the morning strikes made by the Americans on the Luzon airfields. So the Americans were on the attack, he learned. He knew that it would not be long before they would find his force. Then his radar picked up many blips, about 70 miles away. The ships went into their air defense pattern, and the zigzagging became pronounced. Just after 10 o'clock they saw the first wave, 30 planes coming in.

The *Intrepid* airplane that first sighted the Kurita force got on the radio just after 8 o'clock in the morning and reported excitedly:

"The force consists of 4 battleships, 8 cruisers, 13 destroyers, location is south of the southern tip of Mindoro island, the course is 050 and the speed is 10–12, knots. There are no transports in the group and in all a total of 25 warships."

When Admiral Halsey had that information he made sure that all his task group commanders also had it. And then Halsey ordered the commanders to go after the enemy ships. He reiterated his callback to Admiral McCain to stop the trip to Ulithi and stay and fight the battle. He knew that McCain needed fuel, so he made arrangements for him to have an oiler at his disposal the next day.

Shortly after the sighting of the Kurita force, planes from the carrier *Franklin* found the Nishimura force, which included the battleships *Fuso* and *Yamashiro*, the cruiser *Mogami* and the destroyers *Michishio, Yamagumo, Asagumo* and *Shigure* in the Sulu Sea heading for Surigao Strait, about 75 miles east of the Cagayen Islands. The Americans attacked and put a bomb into the battleship *Fuso*, killed a gun crew on the destroyer *Shigure*, and shot down several float planes that had come from the Nishimura ships. Thereafter the admiral had no more aircraft. The American fliers, of course, claimed much more, but that was typical of fliers of all nations. Almost always a cruiser became a battleship in their eyes, and a destroyer was a cruiser. Anything could be a carrier; the Japanese pilots saw carriers almost each time they went out.

Not long after the sighting of the first two forces Admiral Shima's ships were discovered by a bomber of the Fifth Air Force near the Cagayen Islands. The pilot looked down and saw the ships, although he misidentified them as larger than they were. But they were Shima's two heavy cruisers, one light cruiser, and four destroyers.

With all these targets, Admiral Halsey had to make some decisions and he decided to concentrate the Third Fleet's efforts against Admiral Kurita's force, which he quite properly assessed as the largest and most dangerous to the Leyte landings.

At 9:15 planes were taking off from the carrier *Cabot* to go after the Kurita force. Others came from the *Intrepid*. The torpedo bombers climbed to 12,000 feet and flew below the dive bombers, and up on top were the Hellcat fighters for protection against air attack. As it turned out that sort of protection was not necessary any longer because the Japanese air force was now concentrating on attack, not defense. Fighters were too valuable as kamikaze suicide planes to waste on attacks on enemy aircraft.

At a few minutes before 10:30 the pilots saw their quarry: the Japanese ships below in neat formation, in Tablas Strait, east of Mindoro Island. They saw a dozen destroyers surrounding two columns of cruisers with the battleships in the center of the formation.

The air strike commander then instructed his pilots to come in from all sides of the fleet disposition. The torpedo planes were to attack the leading battleship from the starboard side, and the fighters that had no bombs aboard were told to conduct strafing attacks against ships on the right side of the formation.

The radar of the *Yamato* has spotted the American planes first, but the battleship *Kongo* was the first to open fire, and then the others saw the puffs and the planes and began shooting. The Kurita force was moving along at 18 knots.

So the fighters went down first and crossed the Japanese formation in a barrage of antiaircraft fire. They strafed from a height of 3,000 feet and then headed away for the rendezvous to await the others and fly back to the carrier.

One fighter, strafing the *Kongo*, was hit and went into the sea. The pilot did not get out. A torpedo bomber from Squadron 29 made a water landing 10 miles south of Marinduque Island. Two other bombers flew to the spot and orbited until they saw the pilot and his crewmen waving from their rubber boat, but then being low on fuel they had to go back to the carrier.

The torpedo pilots made individual attacks on ships, several of them going after the leading battleship. The dive bombers went in after both big new battleships, the

Yamato and the *Musashi*. As they attacked the Americans saw the results of the attacks of others, bombing hits and torpedo hits on the ships.

The Japanese then saw—or thought they saw—a new danger. The destroyer *Akishino* reported a submarine. It was not surprising, given the experience of the Kurita force in the Palawan Passage a few hours earlier.

The *Noshiro* sighted a submarine. It was all fantasy; no American submarines were in the area. The battleship *Nagato* broke this up with a realistic report. More planes coming in at 1025.

The cruiser *Myoko* was the first to be hit by the American planes. The captain saw the wake of a torpedo and then another, and one of them struck the starboard side, aft. The electrical system began to suffer and so did the engine room. Soon they were flooded and the electrical system broke down. The *Myoko* began to list heavily to starboard. It was decided that she had to head back for Brunei Bay.

The planes finished their attacks and went back to the carriers, but the strikes by the Americans continued. The *Cabot* sent another air strike that afternoon. On the second strike several pilots reported that one of the big battleships was smoking heavily. This was the *Musashi*, which had been torpedoed several times and hit by a number of bombs. On the first strike the *Musashi* had been hit by one bomb and one torpedo, but by noon she took four more torpedoes. She fell out of the formation, accompanied by the heavy cruiser *Tone*. By 1:30 in the afternoon when the air strike from the *Essex* and the *Lexington* arrived, the *Musashi* was 20 miles back from the formation. Then just after 3 P.M. the *Musashi* was found again by the airmen from the *Intrepid*, *Cabot*, *Essex*, *Franklin*, and *Enterprise*. Ten more torpedoes and 17 bombs hit her.

Her commanding admiral, Rear Admiral Toshibei Inoguchi, reported that the ship was becoming unnavigable. Admiral Ugaki told him to beach the battleship, but power lines had ruptured and waterlines were flooding the ship. Her list was more than 20 degrees. Two destroyers came to stand by, replacing the cruiser *Tone*.

Several of the other Japanese ships of this unit were hit. The *Yamato* and *Nagato* each received two bombs and the *Haruna* was damaged by five near-misses, the cruiser *Myoko* was hit by a torpedo and had a propeller shaft damaged, and she had to return to Brunei. The losses were heavy, including the three ships lost in Palawan Passage, but the force was still enormously strong. What impressed Halsey most about the attack was what it did not do. The whole Third Fleet air force had been alerted to these ships and yet only one was sunk in the attack. To Halsey the lack of success pointed up the basic limitation of the air arm in naval warfare.

About an hour after the attacks stopped, Admiral Kurita turned around and seemed to have started back whence he had come. He sent a message to Admiral Toyoda, explaining,

> Were we to have forced our way through as scheduled under these circumstances, we would merely make of ourselves meat for the enemy with very little chance of success to us. It was therefore concluded that our best course was to retire temporarily beyond the range of hostile planes until friendly planes could strike a decisive blow against the enemy force.
>
> It is therfore considered advisable [because of the repeated air attacks with no air defense forthcoming, as had been promised] considered advisable to retire temporarily from the zone of enemy air attacks and to resume the advance when the battle results of friendly units permit.

Repetition is a Japanese method of emphasis. What that message meant was: "Where is my air cover?" Admiral Toyoda could not answer that question and neither could anyone else. In fact there could have been air cover in the Philippines if the army and the navy could have gotten together; the army had hundreds of planes that it was guarding for tactical operations. As the situation grew desperate on the ground as well as at sea, the army would begin bringing these planes forth. But because the army was not used to operations at sea, its effectiveness was always marred. Just now, Admiral Fukudome had shot his wad with the failed major attack of the morning of October 24 on the Task Force 38 ships, and Admiral Ohnishi still suffered from his painful shortage of aircraft.

Admiral Kurita headed back for about four hours. He also sent messages to Manila asking the same question and urging Admiral Fukudome to attack the enemy, and then he suddenly seemed to realize that he had a schedule to make and time was running out. He reversed course again. It was well for his reputation that he had already done so when he received a chiding message from Admiral Toyoda about an hour after turning back to battle. It did not address the question of air cover, but the greater question of serving the Emperor.

"All forces will dash to the attack," it said, "trusting to divine guidance."

Admiral Ugaki, the commander of the battleships, knew all along that Admiral Kurita had no intention of retiring but was trying to escape the constant attack. After all, the Kurita force had just gone through some 250 individual air attacks that day. What Kurita was looking for was some help from the air. Admiral Ugaki did not really expect very much but disaster at this point, particularly after he looked over the ship that had been the mighty *Musashi*—with the *Yamato*, the prides of the Japanese fleet and the most powerful ships in the world.

When we reversed course we passed by *Musashi* my trusted lieutenant, and her damaged appearance was too pitiful for words. All compartments which could be flooded were already flooded. She was listing about 10 degrees to port and though the Imperial Crest was still visible, she was down by the bow. The deck line of the upper deck in front of the turret was barely visible above the surface of the water. She had sustained 11 torpedo hits and several bomb hits. One of the bombs set fire to the ammunition and damaged the rudder and blew away the No. 1 bridge, places on a battleship for which precautions are taken in advance. It is said that this bomb, which hit the radar "bedsprings," wounded Captain Inoguchi, who was in the antiaircraft control station at the time, and completely destroyed the No. 1 bridge and flag plot.

"Make every effort to keep going," was my fervent prayer. Further as the commander of Battleship Division One, I suggested that the bow of the ship be beached temporarily in a spot of suitable depth off a nearby island, and emergency repairs effected. No appropriate words of sympathy immediately came to my mind. Thus we passed *Musashi* and when we reversed course once more, we passed by *Musashi* again near sundown . . .

It would appear that all of *Musashi's* officers and men are remaining at their posts without complaining. I thought that if things remained as they were she might be able to hold out until the following morning. *Tone* [the cruiser that had been left behind with the *Musashi* to guard her and heretofore considered out of the action] is certainly a problem. She requested that she be allowed to join with the force in its penetration and at 6:30 was ordered to rejoin her unit excluding some damage control personnel who remained aboard *Musashi* to help out, all *Maya* personnel who had been accommodated on *Musashi*, were transferred to a destroyer which pulled up alongside. A little over an hour after sundown, a message was received from a destroyer which had been ordered to stand by the stricken ship that at 7:37 *Musashi* listed sharply to 30 degrees.

Captain Inoguchi had followed Ugaki's advice and had run for the shore but had been unable to maneuver because he was afraid to make any change that might cause her to capsize. Her list was too strong, and three of the four engine rooms were flooded. Even the movement on the same course had its evil effect; the bow continued to go down and 20 minutes later Captain Inoguchi gathered his officers and told them to abandon ship, and then went back to his bridge to be alone. But 38 of the officers refused to abandon and many men did not get off either, and when suddenly the *Musashi* rolled over to port and sank, she took down with her 39 officers and a thousand of her 2,200-man crew.

And so Kurita turned back toward San Bernardino Strait. No one saw him, because Admiral Halsey's priorities had suddenly all been changed.

Earlier in the day Admiral Halsey had fretted over the American inability to find the Japanese carriers. As soon as he gathered how important an operation this Japanese move was he knew that the carriers had to play a role in it in some way. But no searches had yet revealed anything about them. By late morning of October 24 in the admiral's plotting room aboard the battleship *New Jersey*, the pieces of the Japanese jigsaw puzzle were coming together. Nishimura, Shima, and Kurita had all been accounted for. But there was something missing. "No operation on such a scale would be undertaken without the use of what the Japanese had left in the way of a carrier force," said Halsey Chief of Staff Robert Carney. "If that carrier force was to be used we felt it would be to the north and east of the Philippines." And so he sent a message in Halsey's name to Admiral Marc Mitscher, the commander of Task Force 38, asking him not to forget the northern area observation flights in the heat of the battle against the known Japanese forces.

Admirals Halsey and Carney thought that probably Admiral Ozawa was again planning to use the shuttle technique that had failed at Saipan. But here in the Philippines with so many more airfields and so many more possibilities, the shuttle technique could be deadly. That is why Halsey wanted so much to find the Japanese carriers, to hit them before they could get involved in shuttling. So the searches to the north went on.

In the middle of the afternoon Admiral Kinkaid had a good picture of what was happening within the Philippine Islands. He knew that three forces of Japanese ships were moving toward Leyte, two of them apparently coming through Surigao Strait and the other one probably heading for San Bernardino Strait, which was the most obvious route from the point where Kurita had been located in the morning. Kinkaid issued orders to Seventh Fleet to prepare for a night engagement, since he estimated that Nishimura and Shima would arrive at Surigao some time during the hours of darkness, after midnight. Admiral Halsey also issued orders to his surface units to prepare for a night fight if Kurita tried to get through San Bernardino Strait.

But by mid-afternoon, it appeared the the Kurita force had taken such a mauling that they were not a major problem anymore. As Admiral Carney, Halsey's staff chief, put it, "they had received so much superficial damage that they were not in a position to render the best account of themselves nor could they be strong enough to gain a decision even if they pressed through the San Bernardino Strait on toward the objective at Leyte."

Then came the reports that Admiral Kurita had turned around and was heading back toward Brunei. In view of all that had happened in the past 36 hours, it seemed quite logical that he might do so, although not very Japanese.

New reports came from Admiral Mitscher. Admiral Halsey had told him to send searches out to the northeast to see if there were other Japanese forces in the area. Just before 4 o'clock in the afternoon one search plane reported seeing three battleships, six cruisers, and six destroyers. Still another search plane in a different area of the northeast reported seeing three carriers, three cruisers, and three destroyers. So there were two more forces, not just one, and Mitscher's pilots had found the elusive Japanese carriers.

Late that afternoon Admiral Halsey was able to come to some conclusions. The manner of the whole Japanese operations suggested a major naval effort. All these forces were proceeding at deliberate speed, as if they had plans to strike simultaneously somewhere. It had to be Leyte, and it had to be on the early morning of October 25.

Halsey assessed the damage his pilots had done to the Kurita force. Three of his task groups each claimed to have damaged the *Musashi*, and one claimed that she was sunk. They also claimed damages to two other battleships, three cruisers, and several destroyers, and Admiral Davison's pilots claimed that three or four ships had been sunk. Altogether it seemed that Kurita had sustained very serious damage. No wonder he had turned around. But later in the evening Halsey learned that Kurita had again turned, this time back to his original course,

Still the damage assessment remained. And there were other factors in Halsey's mind. The Japanese that morning of October 24 had shown that earlier indications that their air strength in the Philippines had been destroyed was an error.

The attacks on the task force ships and the sinking of *Princeton* had indicated that they still had plenty of punch. Halsey had no way of knowing that the one great attack had dissipated most of that newfound air strength. He only could know what he had experienced. He knew the carriers were out there, and he knew the Japanese liked to use the shuttle technique, so he saw a definite threat to the invasion as long as those carriers were afloat.

Halsey's orders from Nimitz were to give assistance to Kinkaid's invasion of the Philippines, but Nimitz also told him that if he had a chance to destroy the Japanese fleet, he should do so. Now in this instance, what was the Japanese fleet? One either had to consider the Kurita force or this new force the more important, and teh indications from the pilots were that the northern force was bigger and more powerful than Kurita's. Besides, it had the carriers, and all during the war the carriers had proved to be the most important elements of the Japanese fleet.

So, having weighed the possibilities, Admiral Halsey decided he would move north at all possible speed and destroy the Japanese carriers with his planes, and if possible their surface forces with his battleships. He estimated that enough damage hed been done to the Japanese Kurita force that Admiral Kinkaid's capital ships and escort carriers could deal with them.

At 8:30 that night Halsey issued orders to the four carrier task groups to move with all speed up north to engage the two Japanese units coming down. The rest of the fleet would go north with them, to find and engage the battleship force that had been reported separately.

Two of Halsey's admirals, Bogan, the carrier man, and Willis Lee, the battleship man, tried to suggest that the Kurita force represented the greatest Japanese threat. But by this time Halsey's mind was made up, and their messages probably did not even get to him but may have been intercepted by the staff.

So the decision was made that set up two of the battles of Leyte Gulf: the destruction of the Japanese carrier fleet off Cape Engano and the battle of Samar.

CHAPTER THIRTEEN

The Decoy

The Japanese psychological estimate of their American enemy was as superb as their strategic estimate was faulty, but given the war situation in 1944 Imperial General Headquarters had only two options: Either keep fighting with the diminishing weapons at hand, or surrender. Given the historical fact that Japan had never been conquered, and given the option of unconditional surrender, which to the Japanese military was unthinkable, there was no option at all. The basic error, recognized before the war by such men as Admiral Yamamoto, had been to start a war that Japan could not possibly win. Now all they could do was delay the inevitable on the off chance that the enemy might tire of the struggle.

In that sense, and given the willingness of the Japanese to sacrifice themselves for country and for emperor, the Sho Operation had a chance of delaying the enemy perhaps for months. Admiral Kinkaid above all was aware of the fragility of the Allied beachhead on Leyte and recognized, as did Admiral Toyoda, that a strong surface attack that wiped out the transports could make the whole Leyte operation untenable.

Admiral Ozawa really expected to sacrifice himself and his ships and men so that the Kurita force could get in among the transports at Leyte and wreak havoc, but he had to play the game as though he had a real chance of victory. If perhaps by some miracle he could bring part of his fleet back unscathed, then he had to have fuel to do so. It was a measure of the Japanese planning at this stage of the war that Admiral Toyoda allowed for a round trip and put tankers at Ozawa's disposal to make that possible. On October 21 the tanker *Takane Maru* and three escort vessels had sailed for Amami o Shima to await the coming of Ozawa on his return trip. On October 23 another tanker, the *Jinei Maru*, had sailed with three escorts. But in mid-voyage one of the escorts had been torpedoed by an American submarine.

Ozawa's sacrifice very nearly did not come off at all. After he sailed from Japan he began to send messages from the flagship *Zuikaku*, fully expecting the Americans to pick up the transmissions and to triangulate his position. But he did not know that the radio system of the *Zuikaku* was faulty and his messages were not getting through. So although he and Admiral Toyoda had hoped that Halsey would be lured away on October 22 or 23, and thus leave a clear field for Admiral Kurita's dash to San Bernardino Strait, it did not happen that way, and it was only by luck that the Ozawa force was sighted in mid-afternoon on October 24. By that time Halsey's planes, which were supposed to have been diverted north before the Kurita dash, had inflicted serious damage on the Kurita force.

By the evening of October 23 Admiral Ozawa was aware that the Kurita force was in trouble already and that the *Atago* and the *Maya* had been sunk and the *Takao* badly damaged. He decided then that he would head for the northern tip of Luzon and that at 6 o'clock on the morning of October 24 he would change course, head southwest, and lure Halsey away from San Bernardino Strait to help Kurita get through. At 5:45 he would launch search planes, and if they found the American fleet, he would send all his air strength in one great wave to attack.

On October 24 Ozawa sent out a search mission early in the morning, and at 8:30 they found the American force. But they also found terrible weather. This disturbed Ozawa more than a little because his new group of carrier pilots were nothing like the old hands; he had little confidence that they could even land successfully on a carrier once they took off. He wanted his single air strike to be as effective as possible, so he waited.

CHAPTER FOURTEEN

The Battle of Surigao Strait

While Admiral Kurita was trying to evade the American attack planes, and Admiral Halsey was trying to find the Japanese carriers, and Admiral Ozawa was frantically trying to be discovered, all that day of October 24 Admiral Kinkaid and the fighting ships of the U.S. Seventh Fleet were gearing themselves up to repel the Japanese invaders heading for Surigao Strait, hoping to round the corner and then join Admiral Kurita on a pincers movement against the American transports and the beachhead in Leyte Gulf.

Off the beaches, Admiral Barbey and Admiral Wilkinson were overseeing the continued supply and management of the naval assistance program to the invading troops. At 8 o'clock in the morning Japanese snoopers began to come around and the ships went to general quarters. A dozen planes appeared, but only about a third of them dropped bombs. Again, these were probably army aircraft, unskilled in attacks on ships, but two bombs hit very close to the *Blue Ridge*, Admiral Barbey's flagship. A few minutes later two more bombs hit between the *Blue Ridge* and the Australian cruiser *Shropshire*, but no damage was done and the bombers were shot down by the planes from the escort carriers.

But there was plenty of air action that day off Leyte to satisfy the most danger-loving, as the diary of Captain Tarbuck of the *Blue Ridge* indicates so much better than the action reports of the day.

Enemy dive bombers launch an attack on the starboard bow. All guns open up with a hell of a roar. The *Shropshire* and a destroyer commence firing also and the aircraft turn away. Fighter pilots can be heard over the radio "tallyhoing" the enemy. Three fall burning and one crashed on shore. One LCI bursts into flames from a hit or plane crash. One liberty ship is hit by a bomb. There is too much smoke to identify ships and the burning oil smoke of the LCI rises five thousand feet. Flames about 200 feet. Our combat air patrol is being relieved by a new group arriving on station from the escort carriers. The support air craft circuit announces the splashing of more than 20 enemy planes . . .

That morning in spite of the air raids, the unloading of supplies by the transports continued on schedule. At that point 141 ships lay in the gulf, a prime target for Admiral Kurita and his ships if they could only get in among "the pigeons." Besides what was in the ships, these and other vessels had landed 144,000 troops and 244,000 tons of supplies. If the *Yamato* could train its 18-inch guns on the shore, the 144,000 men could be made most uncomfortable and the invasion might even fail. It was a grim worry of Admiral Kinkaid's because he felt the responsibility very strongly. He was much comforted by the initial battle plan sent by Admiral Halsey, which showed that Halsey intended to keep the new battleships of the Third Fleet to guard San Bernardino Strait and thus prevent the attempt of Admiral Kurita to break through.

At 3 o'clock in the afternoon another air attack was mounted against the ships in the bay. A twin-engined bomber skidded by the side of the *Blue Ridge* and then a Zero whizzed by on the other side, both of them apparently unhurt by fire from destroyers. But the air cover was effective again and several attacking Japanese planes were shot down by the fighter planes from the escort carriers.

The attacks continued, almost all of them from army planes, and very ineffective for the amount of noise and smoke that was created. But the smoke from burning planes and antiaircraft fire became so intense that on the *Blue Ridge* often they could hear noise but could not see what was causing it.

Ashore, everything was going according to schedule. That evening General Krueger, commander of the Sixth Army, went ashore and set up headquarters, as scheduled. Admiral Kinkaid would have liked to have General MacArthur go ashore, too, so that the *Nashville* could be used in the coming battle with the Nishimura force. But MacArthur was comfortable and did not want to move, so the *Nashville* was ordered to stay out of the fighting.

In the afternoon Admiral Kinkaid got his ships lined up for the night battle. Admiral Oldendorf's old battleships were the key unit for this engagement, but the force also included six battleships, eight cruisers, 26 destroyers, and 39 PT boats.

As darkness came the noncombatant ships assembled in San Pedro Bay. This included the transports and the command ships, because the command ships of the admirals were excellent for communications but not much good in a fight. They had antiaircraft weapons but not much else. And in this instance the *Nashville* had joined that fleet because of its special passenger, General MacArthur.

The tension grew. No one actually knew that Admiral Nishimura was coming down on them, but everyone who had access to naval intelligence suspected. The battle plan called for destroyers on the right and the left, the cruisers behind them, and the battleships on the left and behind Hibuson Island, protected and able to fire over the smaller ships.

By darkness on October 24 the Americans were as ready as they could be, if not as ready as Admiral Kinkaid wanted. The PT boats had let the force down, because of the 50 boats in the fleet only 20 were ready for action that night. The others had sick engines or other maintenance problems, really the result of just getting there and setting up, and there was no one to blame and nothing much to be done but make the best use of the boats available. Or that is what was said, until it was learned in the PT boat force that there was going to be a fight that night. Suddenly the number of operational boats went up to about 40.

One serious problem had developed. The ships were loaded with high-explosive ammunition, laid on for bombardment purposes. No one had anticipated so quick a response by the Japanese fleet, so the battleships had only about enough armor-piercing ammunition to send off five salvos each. This meant that if lesser ships came in the battleships would hold their fire or use high-explosive, saving the armor-piercing for the enemy battle wagons, for nothing else would stop them.

There were some other military problems. The destroyers were short of torpedoes, and they had used up most of their five-inch ammunition bombarding the beaches. All this was understandable but did pose some problems. But to compensate for that, the American position was very strong; the enemy would have to come up in files and the American ships, horizontally across the mouth of the strait, would be able to fire on them from the "crossing the T" position, that most favored of fighting methods.

The battle plan called for the PT boats to engage the Japanese from as far down as the Mindanao Sea. They would harry the enemy all the way to the strait, darting in and out like waterbugs, and then when the Japanese had run that gauntlet the destroyers would launch a torpedo attack. The cruisers and battleships would then take the enemy ships under fire one by one as they came in range.

The Americans were very confident. Admiral Kinkaid suspected that Admiral Nishimura's force had really not been hurt much by the day's attacks, although pilot reports had been glowing about bomb hits and strafing runs.

The Japanese, coming toward Surigao Strait, were already showing the signs of wear and tear. One element that was supposed to be with Admiral Nishimura was Destroyer

Division 23, which was part of the Shima striking force that was to come in just after Admiral Nishimura. The division had first gone to Takao in Taiwan to bring base equipment for the Second Air Fleet and then to join in the Surigao Strait invasion. This division consisted of the destroyers *Wakaba*, *Hatsuharu*, and *Hatsushimo*.

They loaded up in Takao and set out for Manila, arriving on the afternoon of October 23 with the Second Air Fleet material and ground personnel. They were supposed to get out that afternoon but they were delayed in fueling so they did not get away from Manila harbor until later.

On the morning of October 24 they were discovered by the planes of Admiral Davison's carriers, which bombed. The *Wakaba* was hit and near-missed; she became unnavigable and sank before 9 o'clock in the morning. The *Hatsuharu* picked up a handful of survivors, and continued south. But just before noon the *Hatsushimo* was bombed and hurt badly. She could still move at full speed but had lost guns and men. So when another intense bombing raid followed, the two destroyers reversed course and went back to Manila Bay. Their action also helped convince Admiral Halsey that the Third Fleet had indeed dealt heavy blows to the Japanese who were trying to break up the Leyte landing operations, and added to his conclusion that Admiral Kinkaid had plenty of armed might with him to protect the invasion forces.

Also attacked that morning of October 24 were the Nishimura ships, but they steamed steadily toward Surigao Strait. The afterdeck of the battleship *Fuso* was set afire by a bomb, but the fire was extinguished. One observation plane belowdecks was wrecked by that same bomb.

The senior officers of the fleet who knew about the Sho plan in detail had suggested that Admirals Nishimura and Shima should get together and go in as a fleet, but they ran afoul of naval protocol and the fact that Nishimura and Shima really did not like each other very much. Nishimura was more able than Shima, but Shima outranked him in seniority so the doubling up was patently impossible.

After the first air attacks, Nishimura waited for more and was surprised when they did not come. The cruiser *Mogami* sent her search plane out and it found the Seventh Fleet battle force sprawled across Leyte Gulf. The pilot reported four battleships, two cruisers, four destroyers, 15 aircraft carriers, 14 PT boats, and 80 transports. By the time Nishimura got there, he hoped, the carriers would all be gone, heading out to search for Admiral Ozawa. Still the force was very large, and Nishimura was glad that Kurita would be coming down from the north.

The schedule called for Nishimura to reach Dulag at 4:30 in the morning, but he decided to press ahead and get there early.

By midday the damage done in the air attack had been mostly put right. The fires aboard the *Fuso* had been put out, and the gun crew of the number one gun of the destroyer *Shigure*, killed in the blast of a bomb inside their turret, had been replaced. The two ships moved along at 18 knots.

Like Admiral Ozawa, Admiral Nishimura was nonplussed when he received the message stating that Admiral Kurita was turning back from the mission but he kept on at that steady 18 knots, and in late afternoon he was relieved to learn that Kurita had turned around and was making up lost time.

Nishimura pushed on ahead of schedule, and one of his captains said it was because Nishimura was of the Japanese school that preferred to fight night battles against a superior force. Nishimura wanted to be sure that he arrived at Surigao Strait in the nighttime darkness, and not as dawn was breaking. To make doubly sure, he speeded up. At 8 o'clock that night he sent the cruiser *Mogami* and the destroyers *Asagumo, Yamagumo,* and *Michishio* ahead to reconnoiter. He sent a message to Kurita telling him that he intended to reach a point off Dulag at 4:30 in the morning and then begin shooting up the American transports.

Admiral Shima was plugging along behind Admiral Nishimura so far back that he could not help Nishimura in any trouble that might come. Shima had been following all the events and was as thoroughly confused as anyone. He sent a plane to Manila to tell Admiral Fukudome and the army headquarters what he was going to do. His planes were supposed to come back to him but when they reached the Cavite naval bases they were commandeered for search duty and he never saw them again. When he reached Coron Bay as he had been told to, he found no tanker waiting there for him—another sign of the botch-up that Imperial General Headquarters had made of the whole Sho Operation. On the morning of October 24 Admiral Shima finished moving fuel around within his force. He had refueled the destroyers from the cruisers, and that left the whole force with five days of fuel operating at 20 knots.

That morning he wondered what he was going into but did not get any information from anyone. His officers were very discouraged as he set out to follow Admiral Nishimura into Surigao Strait.

Admiral Shima had decided that he would wait several hours after Nishimura had gone through the strait before he would enter and turn up to Leyte to see what Nishimura and perhaps Kurita had accomplished. The flagship would go first, planning to arrive at the strait at 6 o'clock in the morning. If the American ships were there the cruisers would make their attack, followed by the destroyers that would deliver a devastating torpedo volley. Shima then would sweep around the wreckage into the gulf. After knocking off all the remaining transports, he would devote the rest of his ammunition to wrecking the supply dumps on the beaches and then steam triumphantly back to Japan.

Later on October 24 when Shima learned that Nishimura had advanced the time of his attack, he did so, too, to retain the same relative time lag as before. He expected that Nishimura's force would be decimated, but he counted on Nishimura to deal with most of the American ships before he got there.

As Kurita headed for San Bernardino Strait that night he radioed Nishimura and Shima and asked them to arrange their timing so that they could meet Kurita off the southern tip of Samar Island at 10 o'clock on October 25. To comply Admiral Shima pushed his speed up to 22 knots, which was the maximum he could manage and still have enough fuel to get home. Any speed over this would eat up fuel at an alarming rate.

Back in Tokyo that evening, Admiral Toyoda watched the plot of movement of his forces with growing dismay. From the very beginning, he had not felt that the Sho Operation had much chance of success, but the failure of the air forces to perform as expected had been a serious blow to his hopes. As far as he could see the air forces had done nothing: The ships had gotten no assistance at all from the army air force, and Kurita at least had suffered serious damage almost before he got started. His force now was minus one of its greatest weapons, the giant battleship *Musashi*, and had lost two heavy cruisers. Now there came promises from Manila that a new attack would be carried out before dawn of the 25th using heavy bomber, light bomber, and attack forces. But even as the promises were made it was apparent to the pilots on the fields that they could not be kept. There simply were not enough aircraft left in service to do the job.

Admirals Fukudome and Ohnishi were just then meeting at a spot near Manila and arguing about the method they should employ best to serve the cause of Kurita. Fukudome held out for the conventional air attack. Ohnishi said it was impossible, there were not enough aircraft, and the only possible solution to the problem was the kamikaze attack.

The first bit of the gauntlet that the Japanese ships would have to run would be manned by the PT boats. They had been arranged in 13 three-boat sections spread out from Bohol Island to Surigao Strait. At about the time darkness fell Admiral Nishimura's ships were nearing Bohol Island but they saw nothing except a bonfire on the island.

On Bohol PT Boat Section One picked up the Nishimura flagship, the other battleship, and the protecting destroyers, and moved out at 24 knots to attack the behemoths. It was just after 10:30 on the night of October 24. In 15 minutes the forces sighted each other and the battle of Surigao Strait began. The PT boats had two tasks to perform. One was to attack, but the more important task was to inform Admiral Kinkaid of the progress of the enemy. *PT-131, PT-130*, and *PT-152* hastened to do battle and the Japanese destroyers turned on their searchlights and got ready to shoot. The *Shigure*'s shells were bracketing the PT boats, although the boats were zigzagging violently, and soon the boats began making smoke to shield their actions as they tried to get into position to launch an attack. The radio men on each boat were working furiously trying to get the message to Surigao Strait.

The Japanese were good shots. *PT-152* was hit by an explosive shell that blew up her 37-mm gun, killed one man, and wounded three. A shell passed through the hull of *PT-130* but did not explode, and *PT-130*, rushed over to the area occupied by Section two, while the remaining boat still tried to get the message through about the coming of the Japanese, But the Japanese jammed the broadcast and so the message did not get through. The only way the message was passed along was by *PT-130*, carrying it by hand to the next station.

The Nishimura force was now split into two groups, the battleships and destroyers in the south, and the *Mogami* and some other destroyers in the north. The *Mogami* group passed by PT Section Two without being observed. The Nishimura ships moved on, radioing Kurita and Shima that they were moving and destroying PT boats as they went.

Off Limasawa Island the Nishimura force encountered more PT sections. Two boats came out firing torpedoes at the Japanese ships but missed. The destroyer *Yamagumo* started after them but the PT boats wisely fled, and when one of the boats suffered engine failure, it dropped depth charges, which confused the Japanese. The Japanese did not stop to argue, but moved on at 18 knots.

At 1 o'clock in the morning Admiral Nishimura radioed that he would soon pass Panaon Island and that meant he would move into Leyte Gulf through Surigao Strait. He was not sure there were any American ships about, for he had seen no indications of them and had passed only a handful of PT boats as he might have expected to do. He put his fleet into its battle order at this point The destroyer *Michishio* led, followed by the destroyer *Asagumo*, the battleships *Yamashiro* and *Fuso*, and the cruiser *Mogami*, with the destroyer *Yamagumo* on the starboard side and the destroyer *Shigure* on the port.

Admiral Oldendorf was waiting with his battle line. The message given by hand by *PT-130* had reached him just after midnight, so he knew Nishimura was coming and approximately when he would arrive. He waited; there was nothing else to do for the trap was set and only the Japanese could spring it.

They came, at 18 knots, in their formation into the narrow gap that separates Panaon and Sumilon islands and makes the strait. PT Section Six darted into attack position but their torpedoes missed. One after the other, PT sections attacked. The Japanese counter pattern was always the same, and effective. They would turn on the searchlights, try to find the boats, and open fire at anything that moved. The PT boats ran and the Japanese suffered no damage. The PT boats suffered: One was sunk, nine were hit by Japanese fire, and they accomplished nothing as far as they could see. But they had brought the word and they had, like gnats, flown at the enemy and kept him uncomfortable.

The next action was that of Destroyer Squadron 54. That squadron was detailed to make a torpedo attack on the coming Japanese. Two of the destroyers were left to screen transports but the other five would attack in two sections, from east and west.

The destroyer men had been yearning for action ever since the Leyte operation began, but they were employed in the boring duty of escorting vessels here and there and patrolling the strait, without seeing anything but an occasional enemy aircraft in the distance. When the word came down from the top that the destroyers were going into action, everything changed and the atmosphere became electric.

Captain Coward was ready and waiting by 8 o'clock that night. He had informed all his ships that there were no friendly planes operating around the gulf that night, so any planes they saw would be enemy, and they knew what to do. Admiral Oldendorf instructed him to make the attack, count the composition and other details about the enemy, and then retire between Hibuson Island and Dinagat. That way the American battleships and cruisers would know they were coming and would not mistake them for Japanese and begin shooting.

Midnight came and still the Japanese had not. Coffee and sandwiches were served to the men who were at action stations, ready to go. Still nothing.

Then at 10 minutes past one o'clock in the morning PT boats sighted three star shells fired 10 miles away, which could have been flares dropped by an aircraft or a ship signal to other ships. The scene was off the southern tip of Panaon Island, and Admiral Oldendorf sensed that it was meaningful in the extreme. So he passed the word to Captain Coward, and the captain formed up his two groups, sent the destroyers to their stations, and was ready to go.

In a few minutes came another message from Admiral Oldendorf. The enemy had arrived and was trying to drive those PT boats off with gunfire.

Just before 2:30 Captain Coward announced that he was going to start down the strait. The eastern attack group was formed up—the *Remey*, the *McGowan*, and the *Melvin*. The distance between destroyers was 500 yards. They would go in at 20 knots. They were off.

Ten minutes later the Japanese were picked up by the destroyers' radar—two large pips about 18 miles away. The destroyers speeded up to 25 knots and made the torpedo tubes ready. It was to be a straight torpedo attack, run in, fire, and run out; no shooting, because they were up against battleships which outgunned them very heavily and the flashes from their own guns would only make them a target.

By 2:53 the radar operators could see that they faced a seven-ship formation; two big ships, the battleships, and then the smaller cruiser *Mogami* and the four destroyers. A moment later a Japanese searchlight was turned on, made a brief sweep over the *Remey* formation, and was turned off.

The American destroyers began firing torpedoes. They fired on the first target, then switched to the second. The Japanese searchlight came on again, and this time it remained on. The skipper of the *Remey* ordered a full salvo of nine torpedoes fired because he did not know when his ship might become a target and get hit and he wanted to get his attack over with.

A minute later the torpedoes were gone and the *Remey* came around swiftly and headed north into safety and the protection of the American battleships. The destroyers began making smoke to cover their retreat.

From the other side the *McDermut* and the *Monssen* attacked. Here is the recollection of a junior lieutenant, B. F. Goldsworthy, as noted in the ship's action report:

Upon the sounding of the General Quarters alarm at 2:07 I took my battle station as OOD relieving Ensign Begle. The captain had the conn and was stationed on the open bridge forward of the pilot house. I remained in the pilot house.

We were proceeding in a general southerly direction. A group of five destroyers in column were four miles southeast of us. A turn to the left was executed taking us outside and to the east of those destroyers. Standard speed was changed to 20 knots. Shortly we were ordered to steam at 25 knots.

The captain ordered me to go to the open bridge forward of the pilot house and to watch things for a moment. He went to the public address system and spoke to the the crew.

"To all hands. This is the captain. We are going into battle. I know each one of you will do his duty. I promise you that I will do my duty to God and my country. Good luck to you and may God be with us."

The captain then went back to the open bridge and the lieutenant went back to the pilot house.

The captain gave his order to the steersman through the open portholes. These orders were repeated by the chief quartermaster, who remained on the bridge with the captain. He was tired and occasionally he got the orders mixed up but since he repeated what he heard very loudly, this was rectified by the captain who understood the chief's fatigue.

The pips from the enemy ships were now clearly visible, they were off about 12 miles.

When the range closed to about 10 miles I observed lights to port and upon going to the port wing of the bridge I saw two star shells.

While we were going in for our attack, perhaps during the last three minutes, I had the distinct impression that we were being fired upon by the enemy. The basis for this impression is hazy in mind but I seem to recall hearing gunfire and shells whistling overhead and of feeling the ship slightly jarred. I saw sharp flashes of light, although this could have been the result of starshell. The greater part of the time my eyes were on the scope.

Captain Coward reported that we had been straddled. Shortly after that the order was given to fire the fish. Almost immediately Mr. Lawston at the port torpedo director gave the order to fire five. Everything took place similar to the exercises I had seen him conduct many times before. After firing the fish we made rapid turns principally to the right. The order was given by the captain to make all the speed you can. We were illuminated by searchlights which seemed to stay directly on us for only a short time and to sweep back and forth. So I asked the captain if we could not open fire on the ship that was illuminating us. He refused, saying the enemy apparently did not see us as he did not train continually on us.

By this time the Japanese were firing and the destroyers were zigzagging and the shells were landing all around them. On the radar screen the enemy ships moved as though attempting to dodge torpedoes. Aboard the *Melvin* the radar operator suddenly noted that one of the Japanese destroyers had disappeared from the screen.

Twenty minutes later the enemy had ceased fire and the speed of the enemy ships had dropped to 10 knots. Not long after that the destroyers reached Hibuson and Dinagat and came through, and then slowed down and began their patrol duty again. The destroyers had come through without a scratch.

And what had they accomplished?

From about 11 P.M. west of Panaon Island, the Japanese force had engaged a succession of PT boats until about midnight when the battleships came up. Then there was another attack from several torpedo boats at the southern entrance to Surigao Strait and these were brought under fire. The boats fired many torpedoes at the *Mogami* but none of them hit, and neither did any of the battleships or others get hit.

At 2 o'clock on the morning of October 25 the Japanese sighted two American destroyers at about three miles and opened fire on them without using the searchlights. The enemy ships then began making smoke. Ten minutes later a second group of destroyers was seen through the smoke and then more torpedo boats appeared beneath a parachute flare fire by one of the Japanese ships. The Japanese then saw torpedo wakes and began to take evasive action but it was a little bit late for that.

One torpedo slammed into the side of the battleship *Fuso* amidships, causing that ship to slow appreciably and list immediately to starboard. She fell back and the *Mogami* moved up behind the battleship *Yamashiro*. Then the ships were busy moving trying to avoid the torpedoes and thus unable to open fire effectively on the destroyers.

The men on the bridge of the *Mogami* caught sight of the *Asagumo*. Her bow was blown off and she was pouring forth smoke. They saw the destroyer *Michishio* hit by a torpedo that also blew off that ship's bow. They saw the *Yamashiro* hit by another torpedo.

Captain Nishino of the destroyer *Shigure* saw much more.

He saw torpedo attacks delivered from both sides of the Japanese formation. All three of the leading destroyers were hit, and the *Yamagumo* saw the *Michishio* and the *Asagumo* became unnavigable and fall out of the formation. The *Shigure* took evasive action early and avoided all torpedoes.

Admiral Nishimura urged his ships to move forward to the attack, but not many of them were capable of an action at all: one destroyer sunk and two with their bows blown off, and one battleship torpedoed and listing.

In a few minutes fires ate through the bulkheads and blew up the magazine of the *Fuso*, which immediately broke in half and sank, taking down Admiral Masami Ban.

Soon the *Michishio* sank as well, but the *Asagumo* did not; she managed to shore up her broken bow and limped away back toward Brunei.

After the attack by Captain Coward's squadron Destroyer Squadron 24 under Captain K. M. McManes began an attack on the Japanese force. Six more destroyers moved in and fired torpedoes and then opened fire with their five-inch guns. The destroyer *Hutchins* was very nearly hit and the men on the bridge could see the shells "walking down the ladder" toward them, but the last shell hit 50 yards over the ship and the captain changed course to see the next salvo fall in the wake where the *Hutchins* had been a few seconds before. What Captain McManes hit is not very well determined but the destroyer apparently gave the coup de grace to the destroyer *Michishio*, which took several torpedoes from *Hutchins* and blew up.

The Japanese now approached the American battleship line, but there was one more destroyer squadron to be heard from, Captain R. N. Smoot's Destroyer Squadron 56. But their shooting was not very accurate, except for the *Newcomb*. All their torpedoes missed the Japanese and they

retired near Hibuson Island; the *Newcomb* may have scored
hits on the battleship *Yamashiro*. One survivor of that battle
indicated that the *Yamashiro* had taken five torpedoes in the
three destroyer squadron attacks.

On retiring, the last of the Smoot destroyers, the *Albert
W. Grant*, was found by the Japanese guns and hit. Then
she found herself the target of American guns. Altogether
she took 19 hits, 11 of them from American ships, and
soon was dead in the water Her crew suffered 34 killed
and 94 wounded. But the stricken ship was saved when
the *Newcomb* came up, lashed herself alongside the *Albert
W. Grant*, and hauled her clear of the battle zone.

Just before 4 o'clock in the morning, at about the time
Admiral Shima hoped he would be moving off Dulag, the
Nishimura force came under American gunfire from the big
ships. *Yamashiro* was traveling at 12 knots still despite torpedo hits, and so was the cruiser *Mogami* and the destroyer
Shigure. The *Fuso* had sunk but Admiral Nishimura did
not yet know that and was sending messages to that ship
as though she were still fighting.

The battleships *West Virginia, Tennessee*, and *California*
soon had the Japanese under fire, and the *Maryland* and
Mississippi also joined in.

The Japanese were taking a terrible beating from everything from 16-inch shells to six-inch. They fired back, but
except for disabling the *Albert W. Grant* and scoring one
near-miss on the destroyer *Claxton*, the Japanese ships did
not score. The cruisers *Denver, Minneapolis, Columbia*,
and *Portland* were firing on the *Yamashiro* and then on
the *Mogami*; they fired 3,100 rounds. The cruisers *Boise*
and *Phoenix* also fired, and so did the Australian cruiser
Shropshire.

By 4 o'clock the *Yamashiro* was burning brightly along
her entire superstructure. The *Mogami* had turned to retire,
and the *Shigure* retired taking only one hit from an eight-
inch cruiser shell, and that did not explode.

When Admiral Oldendorf learned what had happened
to the *Albert W. Grant* he ordered all the American and

Australian ships to cease fire so the destroyer could be saved. At that point the *Yamashiro* turned and speeded up to 15 knots to retire to the south.

Just before 4 A.M. the cruiser *Mogami* caught fire. Two minutes later a salvo of shells from an American cruiser hit the bridge and killed the captain, the executive officer, and all the others on the bridge. Other shells smashed into the engine room and the fireroom, and the ship slowed almost to a stop.

But the Americans then began to see torpedo wakes of fish fired by the *Mogami*, and Admiral Weyler ordered the battleships to turn north and hold their fire until they had gotten out of danger. During the 10 minutes this took, the *Mogami* turned and escaped and the *Yamashiro* sank.

So, by 4:30 on the morning of October 25, the Nishimura force was no more. The damaged *Mogami* and the almost undamaged *Shigure* were retiring, and the battleships *Fuso* and *Yamashiro* and and the destroyers *Michishio* and *Yamagumo* had been sunk.

CHAPTER FIFTEEN

Shima Arrives

The Nishimura force had met almost total disaster, with two battleships and two destroyers sunk, and one cruiser and one destroyer damaged and moving back without having accomplished anything. The single American ship casualty of the action was the destroyer *Albert W. Grant*, and most of the damage done to her had come through friendly fire from American ships.

Following, but not too close, in Nishimura's wake was Admiral Shima's force, consisting of the cruisers *Nachi* and *Ashigara* and the light crusier *Abukuma* and four destroyers. They came steadily without incident until about 3:15 when the American PT boats off Panaon fired at them and missed. But not long after this, the cruiser *Abukuma* was hit by a torpedo fired by *PT-137*. The odd thing was that the PT boat had fired the torpedo at another destroyer and hit the light cruiser by mistake. The explosion killed 10 men and cut the cruiser's speed to 10 knots. She fell out of the formation.

The Shima force now consisted of two heavy cruisers and four destroyers, moving at 28 knots. She passed what seemed to be two ships on fire—actually the two halves of the wrecked battleship *Fuso*.

At about 4:30 Shima saw what appeared to be two enemy ships and ordered the cruisers to attack with torpedoes. The torpedoes were fired but did not hit anything. Shima could see nothing of the Nishimura force and surmised that it had come to a bad end. He decided to retire and called his four destroyers to come, then turned about and headed south, radioing that he had made his attack and was retiring to plan new tactics.

At 4:30 the force encountered the *Mogami*, which was burning and seemed to be dead in the water. The *Nachi* came too close and collided with her, and the *Nachi's* stern was damaged and her speed reduced to 18 knots. Shima now ordered the *Mogami* and the *Shigure* to join up with his column and started back down the gauntlet.

The American ships now began to chase the enemy. A 5:30 the cruisers on the left reached the point where the *Mogami* and the *Nachi* had collided, and to the south they could see two Japanese ships both on fire, and a third one that appeared undamaged. *Louisville* and *Denver* began firing on one ship, the *Mogami*, but did not sink her. Then they were called back by Admiral Oldendorf, who wanted to concentrate his ships because of the possibility of Admiral Kurita coming through San Bernardino Strait. So they steamed off, leaving the *Mogami* still afloat, still burning, but still alive.

The PT boats had recovered their aplomb after the race of the Nishimura force north and now they harried the Shima force as it came back south. They fired several torpedoes which missed but some of them narrowly, and several PT boats were hit and took casualties.

Admiral Oldendorf then sent two light cruisers and three destroyers under Rear Admiral Robert Hayler to finish off the Japanese cripples. Coming south they encountered the crippled *Asagumo* and began firing on her. She fired back as long as she could against the five ships but finally sank before 7:30 that morning.

But almost immediately the American chasing forces had to suspend activity, for they too were called back by Admiral Oldendorf. By this time Admiral Kurita had broken through the San Bernardino Strait and was heading down on the transports in Leyte Gulf. Another major naval battle seemed to be shaping up.

So the Americans disengaged. This action allowed the *Shigure* to escape the fray, and she headed away as fast as she could go, sending a message to Admiral Toyoda of the disaster that had befallen the Nishimura force.

That morning the escort carriers launched aircraft that pursued the Japanese ships where the American ships had left off. Shortly after 9 A.M. they attacked the *Mogami*, and when they had finished their attacks the ship was dead in the water. The destroyer *Akebono* took off the crew and then sank the hulk of the once-proud cruiser with a torpedo. The *Akebono* limped along, having been torpedoed once, and made a haven at Dapitan on Mindano for a little while. She was later cornered by bombers of the land-based American air force and sunk.

Admiral Shima's ships, now numbering two cruisers and three destroyers, were attacked in the Mindanao Sea by American aircraft, but only the destroyer *Shiranuhi* was damaged. The *Ashigara* escaped to Bacuit Bay in Palawan, where the American planes found her on November 4. The cruiser *Nachi* went to Manila Bay where she was sunk by aircraft on November 5.

Meanwhile the army was making good its promise to fight hard on the shores of Leyte, and a special transport unit, consisting of two light cruisers, a destroyer, and four destroyer transports, landed 2,000 troops at Ormoc on the back side of Leyte on the morning of October 26. Of the whole force that had set out, Nishimura's and Shima's, by the first week of November all that was left of the 17 ships were the heavy cruiser *Ashigara* and five destroyers.

CHAPTER SIXTEEN

The Battle of Samar

Admiral Kurita was suffering from an almost complete failure in Japanese communications. He did not know what the naval air forces were up to in Manila. He did not know what had happened to Admiral Nishimura and Admiral Shima. He did not know where Admiral Halsey was with the U.S. Third Fleet, and believed they were about 80 miles off the coast of Samar Island northeast of Leyte Gulf.

Admiral Kurita was also troubled by the situation of his task force. He had lost 10 of the 32 ships that had set out from Brunei Bay. The air attacks of October 24 had cost dearly on the *Yamato*, although structurally she was unharmed. But her communications system had been partially destroyed and could not be repaired until the ships got into port.

Late that night of October 24 Admiral Kurita had sent a message of reassurance to Admiral Toyoda, who seemed to be questioning either his bravery or his judgment.

"This fleet intends to charge into Leyte Gulf at 11 o'clock in the morning, on the 25th without regard for any damage we may suffer," he said, "chancing annihilation." He was hoping against hope for a better performance of the naval air force on the 25th than they had given him on the 24th, but he had no communications with either Admiral Fukudome or Admiral Ohnishi to guide him.

At midnight on October 24 Admiral Kurita's striking force passed through San Bernardino Strait and turned south, hugging the shore of Samar and planning to reach the Leyte beaches at 10 A.M. As day broke at 6:40 the lookouts aboard the Japanese ships sighted carriers on the horizon and watched as they launched planes.

The Japanese ships were moving in four columns. On the east was the destroyer screen, led by the light cruiser *Noshiro*, then the heavy cruisers *Kumano, Suzuya, Chikuma*, and *Tone*. Next to them were the heavy cruisers *Haguro* and *Chokai*, followed by a destroyer squadron led by the light cruiser *Yahagi*. Five kilometers behind was the battleship force: the *Yamato* with her 18-inch guns, the *Nagato* with 16-inch guns, and the *Kongo* and the *Haruna* with 14-inch guns.

A few moments later some of the aircraft approached the Japanese fleet and the ships opened fire on them. The Americans heard and saw the antiaircraft fire and at 6:45 the escort carrier *Fanshaw Bay* had an unidentified ship contact on the radar screen, and the radio watch heard people speaking Japanese. At 6:47 the pilot of one of the antisubmarine patrol planes saw below him four Japanese battleships, eight cruisers, and a number of destroyers, and he made a gliding attack with depth charges and drew antiaircraft fire. He reported to the ship and was warned to check the identification of the ship he was attacking, because Admiral Sprague thought he must be attacking part of Task Force 38 which was supposed to be up in that area.

But in a few seconds lookouts spotted the peculiar pagoda masts that represented the heavy Japanese ships built in the 1930s, and if that were not enough, splashes from Japanese color-coded shells began hitting the water astern of Taffy Three, Rear Admiral Clifton Sprague's command of six small carriers.

Admiral Kurita ordered a general attack, and at 6:48 the Japanese opened fire on Taffy Three. Admiral Sprague ordered his ships to change course, keeping into the wind as was necessary for launching aircraft, but running away from the enemy. Soon the little carriers were making their best speed, 17.5 knots, which was in no way enough to escape that Japanese force that could manage 30 knots if necessary.

Admiral Sprague also called for help in plain English, giving course and speed and asking anyone in the area to give assistance. His message was really directed at Admiral Oldendorf, who commanded the Seventh Fleet battle squadron.

Admiral Thomas Sprague, who was in command of all the escort carrier units, asked for and received Admiral Kinkaid's permission to launch all available aircraft to attack the Japanese fleet. Within 10 minutes the planes were moving toward the enemy. Meanwhile the Japanese ships were moving closer to the escort carriers, which were running ahead of them and heading for Leyte Gulf.

The six carriers of Taffy Three formed a rough circle and launched their planes. The Japanese fire kept coming closer, and three different 14-inch salvos from the battleships straddled the carrier *White Plains* within four minutes. The last straddle was so close it threw men off their feet on the flight deck and knocked out the electrical system for a few seconds, so that steering control was lost, but almost immediately regained as the circuit breakers were snapped back on.

The Japanese fire was coming closer and closer to the ships, and Admiral Clifton Sprague wondered how long they could possibly survive. He ordered his destroyers and destroyer escorts to make a torpedo attack on the Japanese ships and kept launching all available aircraft as quickly as possible, some of them without adequate fuel or armament.

Here is the recollection of Rear Admiral Tomijii Koyanagi, chief of staff to Admiral Kurita, of this phase of the battle:

> The enemy withdrew, first to the east, next to the south, and then to the southwest, on an arc-like track. In retreat he darted into the cover, local squalls and

destroyer smoke screens, while attacking us continuously with destroyer torpedo and attack planes.

Our fast cruisers, in the van, were followed by the battleships and little heed was paid to coordination. Because of the enemy's efficient use of squalls and smoke screens for cover, his ships were visible to us in the *Yamato* only at short intervals. The enemy destroyers were multifunneled with high free board. Their appearance and torpedo firing method convinced us that they were cruisers.

The *Yamato* speeded up. Admiral Kurita estimated that he was facing four or five fast carriers, guarded by at one or two battleships and at least 10 heavy cruisers. Even with such a large force he found it not at all surprising that the carriers would be running away. "Nothing is more vulnerable than an aircraft carrier in a surface engagement so the enemy lost no time in retiring," said Admiral Koyanagai.

Kurita lost no time in sending a message to Admiral Toyoda, announcing his attack had begun.

"By heaven sent opportunity we are dashing to attack the enemy carriers," he said. "Our first objective is to destroy the flight decks and then the task force."

Admiral Ugaki, the commander of the battleships, was frustrated by the excellent use of squalls and smoke by the retreating Americans.

"We hoped to destroy the enemy at one blow if he came out from behind the smoke. In the meantime we were attacked by enemy aircraft. Several salvos from medium caliber enemy guns fell near *Yamato* and two shells hit the starboard after gallery and the outer boat shed."

Those shells had come from the destroyer screen of Taffy Three, which Admiral Sprague had ordered to attack the enemy and thus slow him down. The screen consisted of three destroyers—the command ship *Heermann*, the *Johnston*, and the *Hoel*—and four destroyer escorts—*Dennis*, *John C. Butler*, *Raymond*, and *Samuel B. Roberts*.

The destroyers had the order at 7:16 and broke off the task they were doing so effectively, laying a smokescreen. The *Johnston*, which was nearest the enemy, was already firing, and it must have been her five-inch shells that damaged the mighty *Yamato*. But most of her shells were aimed at the heavy cruiser *Kumano*, which was out in front of the Japanese force, and she fired more than 200 rounds, making many hits. This activity made the *Johnston* the target of all the Japanese cruisers. Then when the order to make a torpedo attack came, the *Johnston* swung around to comply and closed at 25 knots to within six miles of the nearest cruiser and fired 10 torpedoes. Then, having spent all her torpedoes, the *Johnston* turned sharply and retired, making a smokescreen to shield her movements. As she went her crew heard underwater explosions. When they emerged from the smoke they saw the result: The leading Japanese cruiser, the *Kumano*, was burning astern. The commander of that cruiser division, Admiral Shiaishi, then moved his flag to the cruiser *Suzuya*, which had been bombed by the planes of the escort carriers, and the two cruisers moved out of the fight.

But the *Johnston* had claimed the full attention of several Japanese ships. Soon she was hit in quick succession by three 14-inch battleship shells and three 6-inch shells from a cruiser. The explosions knocked out the after engine room and fireroom, the steering engine, and the five-inch guns aft. The destroyer speed dropped to 17 knots, the radar came tumbling down, and great holes were blasted in the deck. Many men were killed by the exploding shells. Steering was shifted to manual. Luckily the rain squall that had hid the carriers for a while now descended on the *Johnston* and gave her a 10-minute respite from the fight. The captain of the ship, Commander E. E. Evans, had two fingers of his left hand blown off and all his clothing above the waist, but he could still fight, and so could his ship.

The next destroyer to act against the Japanese was the *Hoel*. Commander L. S. Kintberger made an approach on the nearest battleship, the *Kongo*, and the destroyer bravely opened gunfire with her five-inch guns. The *Kongo* replied with her 14-inch guns. Soon she took a hit from the battleship that destroyed the voice radio. She fired five torpedoes at the *Kongo*, but the battleship managed to turn and evade them all. Then the *Hoel* began taking hits in the fireroom which jammed the rudder, and knocked out the port engine. The rudder jammed and she steered straight for the enemy battleship.

Now she approached the Japanese cruiser *Haguro*, attempting to torpedo that ship. She launched torpedoes from about four miles away. They ran straight, and the crew of the *Hoel* saw columns of water at the side of the *Haguro* when they were supposed to go off.

The *Heermann* got into action next and launched seven torpedoes at the *Haguro*, which missed. The *Haguro* then was shooting at the *Heermann* but also missed.

As the torpedoes were launched the men of the destroyers saw splashes of 14-inch shells from the *Kongo* tearing up the water all around her. The *Haruna* then appeared astern of the *Kongo* and the captain of the *Heermann* decided to fire the rest of his torpedoes at the *Haruna*. The destroyer fired three torpedoes, thought that one hit, and whipped around to race back to the American formation.

The *Yamato*, beset by torpedoes on both sides, turned and ran with them for 10 minutes before they ran their course, a maneuver that took her out of the battle, fortunately for the American carriers.

The American destroyer *Hoel*, which was running on one engine and half-crippled in every way, tried to retire to the southwest, but she could not move fast enough to get away from the Japanese ships that fired at her constantly She managed to keep going for an hour but she took over 40 shells, from 16-inch to five-inch and soon was full of holes below the waterline. Finally at 8:30 a shell knocked out the remaining engine and the destroyer went dead in the water. The captain warned everybody to prepare to abandon the ship. The firemen readied the plant so no underwater explosions would occur, and the men began to get off. The ship kept afloat for another 20 minutes, the Japanese firing on her all the time, until at 8:55 she rolled over and sank.

Next came the destroyer escorts, which really had no experience in mounting a combined torpedo attack and very little experience in the use of torpedoes at all, although they carried them.

Just before 8 o'clock that morning Admiral Sprague ordered the second torpedo attack. The destroyer escort *Samuel B. Roberts* responded, along with the *Hoel* and the *Heermann*. The *Johnston*, which had no torpedoes left, also traveled toward the Japanese to deliver covering fire.

The *Samuel B. Roberts* was able to approach the heavy crusier column without being seen, largely because of the smoke laid by the destroyers. She came up to within 4,000 yards, just a bit over two miles away from the leading Japanese cruiser, and fired three torpedoes. None of them hit, so she started firing her five-inch guns. She was not hit by enemy shells although she was certainly in range.

The destroyer escort *Raymond* also attacked. Her target was the *Haguro*, which began shooting at her. She launched three torpedoes at the cruiser, but the *Haguro* took evasive action and the torpedoes all missed. The *Raymond* then retired, pursued by eight-inch shells from the cruiser.

The destroyer escort *Dennis* also attacked the *Haguro* and dodged the cruiser's shells and a handful of torpedoes. She launched her own torpedoes at the cruiser *Chokai*, and they missed. She then began firing her guns and turned and dashed back into the formation.

At about 8:30 the destroyers and destroyer escorts that were still navigable moved back to protect the escort carriers with smoke. From time to time one of the ships was hit. The Japanese fire was unending that morning; the *Dennis* took a shell that passed through her deck and passed through the starboard plating three feet above the waterline without exploding. But ten minutes later she was hit again twice, and her number one 5-inch gun was wrecked. The *Samuel B. Roberts* then became a target for the Japanese cruisers. She was hit several times in rapid succession. Apparently two or three 14-inch shells hit all at once and tore a great hole in the ship 30 feet long and seven feet high. The number two engine room was wiped out, and the ship became a mass of battered metal. All power was lost and communications were lost. The order was given to abandon ship but many did not hear it. The ship was abandoned by a few minutes after 9:30 and sank just after 10 o'clock.

Of her crew of eight officers and 170 men, three officers and 86 men were killed in this action.

The *Heermann* also came under attack from the cruiser *Chikuma*, which hit her with a series of eight-inch shells. She was hard hit but continued to fire. The *Chikuma* turned away, but the *Tone* took her place working over the *Heermann*. But the *Tone* also came under heavy attack from the escort carriers and was hurt enough that she fell in astern of the *Haguro* and retired from the battle.

By this time the *Hoel* had been abandoned and the *Samuel B. Roberts* was burning. Now the Japanese destroyers organized a torpedo attack on the American vessels. Seeing this developing, the *Johnston*, which had no more torpedoes, went after the five Japanese destroyers. By doing so she made herself their target and was hit numerous times, but the Japanese destroyers and the cruiser *Yahagi* all turned away. The Japanese destroyers fired torpedoes but they did not reach their targets, which were the escort carriers of Taffy Three.

Those carriers were a tempting target, but the Japanese by this time were very cautious because they thought they were fighting heavy cruisers and light cruisers and destroyers.

"We pursued them for over two hours," said Admiral Koyanagi, "but could not close the gap: in fact it actually appeared to be lengthening." This was very strange since the top speed of the little carriers was 18 knots and the top speed of the Japanese force was at least in the high twenties. But the Japanese estimated the American speed at 30 knots, and Kurita felt he was going that fast, too, using fuel at an enormous rate. If these were fleet carriers as he thought, he might never catch them.

The escort carriers of Taffy Three were constrained by the presence of Taffy Two to the south of them. Therefore they had to zig and zag but not overrun Taffy Two and bring Japanese destruction to them, too. For protection the escort carriers each had one 5-inch gun, and that was virtually the armament, except for antiaircraft guns.

The *Kalinin Bay* was the first carrier to be threatened. She was one of the last ships in the formation, and she was having engine trouble that caused her crew to make emergency repairs so she could keep up. Just before 7:30, with Japanese shells falling all around, she began to launch her planes. She was first hit by the Japanese just before 8 A.M., and she was hit 15 times in all before the Japanese broke off the action. She was lucky; the Japanese were shooting armor-piercing ammunition that usually went right through the little carrier's decks without exploding. But other shells did great damage. Two shells penetrated below the waterline and caused flooding to the depth of five feet. One exploded in the port aviation lubrication oil tank, flooding the forward engine room. One wrecked the machine shop, which flooded to a depth of 10 feet. One exploded under the fantail, smashing the sprinkler system and doing some structural damage. One shell put the elevator out of commission, One smashed the radio room. One made mincemeat of the flight crew locker amidships. Most of the shells were eight-inch. But because the Japanese thought they were facing cruisers and fleet carriers they used armor-piercing ammunition and not the high-explosive that would literally have blown the little carrier out of the water.

The *Fanshaw Bay*, which was in the first line of carriers on the starboard side, was hit by a six-inch shell first, just before 9 o'clock that morning, and altogether by four shells and near-missed by two others. Again she was lucky that most of the shells were armor-piercing so only four men were killed and five wounded, while the *Kalinin Bay* had five killed and 55 wounded. The *White Plains*, which was in the center of the formation of carriers, was not hit at all, but the *Kitkun Bay* saw eight salvos from Japanese ships land all around her, one of which landed 50 yards astern. The *St. Lo* was straddled half a dozen times and saw some near-misses.

And then there was the *Gambier Bay*.

She was on the windward side of the carrier formation, which meant that the smoke blew away from her very quickly, making her the most visible of all the carriers. For half an hour she chased salvos, which meant that her captain kept turning to avoid being bracketed by the enemy ships. But at 10 minutes after 8 o'clock that morning the ship took its first blow, and thereafter the shells falling on the flight deck were like rain. She was being fired on by at least three of the Japanese cruisers.

The carriers, of course, were the primary targets of the Japanese, and the destroyers and escort vessels were simply a nuisance that kept them from getting at the carriers. Ten minutes after the first shell hit the *Gambier Bay* came the shell that really did her in. It landed short of the ship, hit the water just off the port side, and exploded so near the engine room that the plates buckled and the forward engine room flooded. This cut the carrier's speed from 19 to 11 knots, and she then did not have a chance of getting away. From that point on the ship was hit at least every other minute until 9:10, when she sank.

So there were the major casualties of the battle of Samar: the carrier *Gambier Bay*, the destroyer *Hoel*, the destroyer *Johnston*, and the escort *Samuel B. Roberts*. Surprisingly, almost at the precise moment that the *Gambier Bay* sank, Admiral Kurita called off the pursuit of the carriers and ordered all his ships to close up and head back through San Bernardino Strait.

What had caused this remarkable maneuver, giving up the mission that would almost certainly have succeeded in part?

Or would it have?

For despite Admiral Kurita's mistaking the gallant destroyers and escorts for cruisers, so brave was their attack against impossible odds, the Americans had a great deal of strength almost readily available.

The destroyers and escorts had stalled the Japanese attack and given the Japanese pause. The airmen did as much or more. Every available plane of the three groups of the escort carriers was sent aloft to fight the battle. To be sure, some of the planes did not have adequate gasoline, some were not prearmed, but many of them were fueled and armed. Taffy Two, for example, sent three air strikes totaling 36 fighters and 43 torpedo bombers against the Japanese in an hour and half. They dropped 49 torpedoes and claimed 11 hits, all but one on battleships and heavy cruisers. The 55 fighters that went into action dropped 133 armor-piercing 500-pound bombs, hundreds of 100-pound antipersonnel bombs, and 276 rockets. Other planes from Taffy Three and Taffy One also attacked and did considerable damage to several of the cruisers. The *Chikuma* was knocked out and sank not long afterward. In all this Taffy Two used 12 bombers and 111 fighters. Taffy Three lost more planes, but how many more is still not known because the *Gambier Bay* figures are clouded by the loss of the ship.

The planes from the escort carriers attacked like gnats, usually in no sort of formation or with any plan, for there was no time to make a plan, so quickly had the hysteria descended with the appearance of the Japanese battle force.

After Admiral Kurita stopped the pursuit of the escort carriers, on the basis that they were going to get help from somewhere, he milled around for several hours, indecisive. He knew there was a big American force somewhere, and he thought he had been attacking one of the task groups of the Third Fleet, in which case there were two more task groups, hundreds of planes, and a battleship fleet as well to be faced. He sent two float planes down to Leyte Gulf for a look, but neither of them returned, which again gave him pause.

Meanwhile battle damage reports began to accumulate for Kurita. *Yamato* had been hit several times by bombs but they had not done much damage. The cruiser *Chokai* was very badly damaged; later that day her crew was taken off by a destroyer and she was sunk. The cruiser *Suzuya* was attacked again by the American aircraft and a bomb started fires that approached her torpedo storage. She became unnavigable. The crew abandoned and she sank, the third of the heavy cruisers to be lost that day.

And so finally after 1 o'clock on the afternoon of October 25, Admiral Kurita did turn north. He radioed Combined Fleet headquarters that afternoon that he had abandoned the mission against the transports but was heading north to attack another enemy force and then would pass through San Bernardino Strait.

Admiral Ugaki, the commander of battleships in the force, did not agree with Kurita's decision at all. He did not argue with what he saw as the timidity of his superior, but confided his thoughts to his diary:

If battles could be waged by hard and fast rules, there would be nothing to them. At times, however, there are errors and unforeseen events. In particular with the friendly air forces carrying out the attack, I thought that we should have at least pursued the enemy. In general, the will to fight and the ability to act promptly are not all that they should be, and standing on the same bridge I have experienced considerable irritation. If fuel is the primary consideration then it is only natural that we head for San Bernardino Strait. But if the enemy is destroyed, then you can fuel the destroyers from the battleships at night . . .

So Admiral Kurita abandoned the Leyte attack altogether. At 9 o'clock that night he was in the strait and on his way toward safety, it appeared.

It was also apparent that night that the Sho Operation had failed completely and done nothing but cost the Japanese the basic strength that remained of their navy. Nishimura and his ships had been decimated at Surigao Strait, and so had Shima and his vessels. Kurita had lost ships all along

from the Palawan Passage to the waters off Samar, and the
great battleship *Musashi* was the most spectacular victim.
The army generals who opposed the plan argued that to risk
the fleet as the navy had insisted was to lose the fleet.

Now, with the navy's carriers and surface arms in complete disarray, the naval high command would have to come
up with something else to continue the struggle against the
enemy.

CHAPTER SEVENTEEN

The Kamikazes

Even as the American force of escort carriers off Samar Island was menaced by Admiral Kurita's battleships and cruisers, those carriers were coming under attack from the entirely new weapon of the war, the Japanese suicide planes.

For four days since Vice Admiral Takejiro Ohnishi had first proposed the idea of suicide crashes against enemy warships at Mabalacat airfield, Lieutenant Seki, the first pilot to volunteer for a suicide mission, had flown out to blow himself up and an enemy ship to boot, only to be frustrated by weather or failure to find the enemy ships. Four times he had returned. But he was still eager to try again. On October 25 Lietenant Seki's five-man Shikishima unit flew off from Mabalacat at 7:25 in the morning to search for enemy ships in the waters east of the Philippines. If they did not find any they would return to Leyte Gulf, which they knew was full of Allied transports.

But even as the Shikishima fliers left Mabalacat near the Clark Field complex, six army planes from Davao were attacking the escort carrier force to steal Lieutenant Seki's thunder and become the first kamikazes to strike. The carrier *Santee*, a part of Taffy One, which was under direct command of Rear Admiral Thomas Sprague, had just finished launching 11 torpedo bombers and 17 fighters to help Taffy Three which was under attack by the Kurita force.

At 7:40 the carrier was recovering planes sent on earlier missions when it was attacked by the six Japanese planes from Davao. The first came down out of a cloud, starting the dive so close to the aircraft carrier that there was no time to bring antiaircraft guns to bear on it. It came in strafing, crashed into the flight deck on the port side, and continued through the hangar deck. It blew a hole 15 by 30 feet in the deck and started fires near the bomb-stowage compartment. Sixteen men were killed and 27 were wounded in the attack. Damage control parties rushed to the hangar deck and managed to get the fires under control so they did not reach the bombs.

Then, 30 seconds after the first plane came in on *Santee*, another kamikaze attacked the *Suwannee*. When hit by antiaircarft fire it spiraled into a dive and made for the *Sangamon*. The plane was hit by heavy antiaircraft fire and swerved and crashed into the sea. But at the same time a third kamikaze came down on the *Petrof Bay* and was barely knocked out by antiaircraft fire.

At this time the *Santee* was also attacked by the Japanese submarine *I-56*, which put a torpedo into her, but she was well compartmentalized and able to survive the damage. The fourth kamikaze went for the *Suwannee*. That plane was hit by antiaircraft fire, but the pilot had already started his dive and the plane hit the carrier forward of the after elevator, making a 10-foot hole in the flight deck. The bomb exploded between flight and hangar decks and caused many casualties. Fires were started but they were quickly put out. Two hours after this first attack, Lieutenant Seki's Shikishima kamikaze unit found Taffy Three, which had hardly recovered from the scare thrown into it by the Kurita assault. Following Admiral Ohnishi's instructions, these kamikazes had come in just above the surface of the sea, and so their approach did not show on the radar screens.

Lieutenant Seki made the first attack, according to Chief Warrant Officer Hiroyoshi Nishizawa, one of three pilots who had accompanied the Shikishima unit to observe its attack and report back to Admiral Ohnishi. Seki dived into the *Kitkun Bay*, flagship of Admiral Ralph Ofstie. He aimed for the bridge but missed, passed over the island, crashed into the port catwalk, bounced off, and fell into the sea, but the bomb he carried exploded, causing a good deal of damage.

Then two other planes attacked the *Fanshaw Bay*, but both were shot down. The fourth and fifth members of the Shikishima unit started to attack the *White Plains*. They were taken under fire by the ship's 40-mm antiaircraft guns, and one was hit and began to smoke. The pilot pulled around and dove into the carrier *St. Lo*, crashed through the flight deck, and exploded below. Huge sections of the flight deck were flung into the air, and whole airplanes followed. The ship caught fire in a dozen places and soon was blazing from stem to stern and sank in a cloud of smoke and steam.

Thus was the new Japanese weapon forged and tested.

CHAPTER EIGHTEEN

The Phantom Carriers

The Japanese called the Ozawa command the main body, but that was a misnomer. What had gone forth from Japan to lure Admiral Halsey away from Leyte Gulf was the ghost of a carrier fleet.

To be sure, the *Zuikaku* was there. She was the last of the proud carriers with which Japan had begun the war. Her half-dozen equals had all been sunk, at Midway and in the battle of the Philippine Sea. Now as companions she had the light carrier *Zuyiho* and the converted seaplane carriers *Chitose* and *Chiyoda*. They called it Carrier Division Three, but it did not deserve the name. Altogether the four carriers could boast of only 80 fighters and 36 bombers.

Carrier Division Four, under Rear Admiral Matsuda, consisted of the converted battleships *Hyuga* and *Ise*. They had two light cruisers and nine destroyers.

Certainly compared to the 32 ships that set out under Admiral Kurita, this was anything but a main force, but the fact that six of the ships were "carriers" was convincing to Admiral Halsey that this was the main force of the Japanese fleet.

Against this sad array of 17 ships, without adequate fuel or adequate aircraft and trained pilots, unable to carry out the tasks that in the early days of the war had seemed so easy, Admiral Halsey brought 64 ships of Task Force 38. The Japanese carriers, having sent off their planes on that abortive mission of October 24, now had only 29 planes aboard all the carriers. The *Intrepid* alone carried 98 aircraft, and it was only one of nine carriers involved (Admiral McCain's task group was not involved in this battle).

Just before midnight on October 24 the three task groups involved met and headed north. At midnight the *Independence*, which was a night carrier, launched search planes to the north, and shortly after 2 o'clock in the morning one of these planes made radar contact with enemy ships, and half an hour later made contact with a second group of ships. The enemy was only 80 miles away.

But then the aircraft that had found and tracked the Japanese broke down with engine trouble and had to return to the *Independence*. The other night search planes never made contact again with the Japanese, and so Task Force 38 was unable to make a night attack or a dawn attack from short range.

In the morning it all started over again.

Halsey's battle plan called for the battleships and cruisers to get out ahead of the carriers, so that when the carrier planes struck in the morning hours, the surface vessels could rush in and finish the job.

But the whole plan was set off balance by the loss of contact. Just before 6 o'clock that morning of the 25th the planes were on deck again and began taking off around 6 o'clock to search out the enemy.

Then Admiral Mitscher did not wait but launched his attack force immediately and ordered them to take station 50 miles ahead of the task force and wait for the reports of the searchers before heading into attack. The reason for this approach was learned at the battle of the Philippine Sea, when the Japanese had the edge by getting in the first strikes before the Americans had found their force. This time Mitscher wanted to be sure that the Americans struck first. Another reason was the lesson learned from Midway: The Americans did not want to be caught with their planes on deck as Admiral Nagumo had been on that fateful day. These preparations were a measure of the American respect for the Japanese enemy, a respect that this day was not warranted by the situation: Admiral Ozawa could not put up 30 aircraft to oppose the Americans. His mission, indeed, was becoming as it had been designed: a suicidal venture, with its successful drawing of the American air fleet away from Leyte.

But that was not really the case. The Seventh Fleet, augumented by the escort carriers, had proved itself quite adequate to defend the landings at Leyte. The loss of an escort carrier, two destroyers, and a destroyer escort was not a high price to pay for the sinking of two cruisers and the damaging of several more to the extent that Admiral Kurita gave up his mission, That is what the Seventh Fleet had accomplished on October 25.

At 7:30 that morning of October 25, the search planes found the Ozawa force once again: Ozawa himself with the *Zuikaku*, three light carriers, two battleship-carriers, light cruisers, and the destroyers.

The carrier planes, having found the Japanese fleet, began to attack and continued to attack. The first wave was met by about 20 Japanese fighters, which was all Admiral Ozawa had. The Americans shot down 11 of them and then after the first wave of attack, spotted more and shot down more.

The American planes found the antiaircraft fire much more intense than the fighter activity for reasons they did not understand.

The first strike put a bomb into *Zuiho* and so many into *Chitose* that she sank. The *Zuikaku* was hit by one torpedo, and that hurt her so badly that she became hard to steer and developed a sharp list. At 11 that morning Admiral Ozawa shifted his command to the *Oyodo*. The destroyer *Akitsuki* was sunk instantly by one torpedo, and by the end of the attack, when Ozawa counted his aircraft, he found he had only six left.

The second strike arrive at about 10 that morning. At that same time Admiral Davison's task group spotted about 25 blips on the radar screen. These could not have been Ozawa's planes; he did not have any. They might have been Admiral Fukudome's but just as likely they were army planes, and this idea was reinforced by their behavior when the combat air patrol came out to meet them: The Japanese turned back, which was quite unlike even the most inexperienced naval pilots to do.

At about this time, too, Admiral Halsey became aware of what was going on back at Samar, where the escort carriers were under attack from Admiral Kurita. He had no very clear picture because the messages that came to him were out of sequence but he got many messages from Kinkaid, asking where was the battleship force that was supposed to be protecting San Bernardino Strait.

That was so long ago, that battle plan, that Halsey had difficulty making out what was meant. He ordered Admiral McCain's group, which was returning to the fray from an aborted resupply trip to Ulithi, to speed to Leyte and engage the enemy. That, he felt, was quite enough. Then he went back to the process of destroying the Ozawa fleet.

In the second air strike the Americans had a field day. They were virtually no Japanese fighters left in the air to cause them trouble. To be sure, the antiaircraft fire was intense, but in previous battles that had been only half the problem. The planes of the *Lexington* and the *Franklin* made bomb hits on the *Chiyoda*, and that carrier burned briskly, listing, and flooded. Her engines quit after a bomb hit just after 10 A.M. The *Hyuga* started to try to tow the *Chiyoda*, but then air strike number three came in and *Hyuga* was busy trying to defend herself. Admiral Matsuda ordered the *Isuzu* and the destroyer *Maki* to take off the crew of the *Chiyoda* but they, too, were so beleaguered they could not. So the *Chiyoda*, in sight of all, was abandoned to her fate and floated helplessly throughout the battle with no rescue for the crew. She was torpedoed late in the afternoon by American cruisers when they arrived on the scene to clean up the cripples.

On this third strike, the planes found a destroyer leading the carriers *Zuikaku* and *Zuiho* with another destroyer on each side and one bringing up the rear, and then the carrier battleship *Ise* behind them. Behind the *Ise*, about 20 miles, was the light cruiser *Tama*, which had already been damaged and was leaking oil. South of her the *Hyuga* and a destroyer were circling the *Chiyoda*, which was dead in the water. To the south were two light cruisers, one damaged and the other circling, and a destroyer that was dead in the water.

The third strike, which arrived over the Japanese ships shortly after 1 o'clock in the afternoon, was very large, consisting of more than 200 planes from the eight carriers of Admiral Davison's group and Admiral Sherman's group. They put three torpedoes into *Zuikaku* simultaneously, and they torpedoed and bombed *Zuiho*. Both carriers began to burn. Forty planes attacked *Zuiho* just after 1 o'clock, and 20 minutes later another wave came in.

Zuikaku sank at about 2:15, and now the force shrank rapidly. The ships around *Chiyoda* abandoned her to fate.

Strike number four consisted of about 15 torpedo planes, half a dozen dive bombers, and about 15 fighters which hit the Japanese again just before 3 P.M. They concentrated on the *Ise* and the *Zuiho*. The *Ise* was almost unhurt but the *Zuiho* sank at about 3:30.

A fifth strike was sent off and arrived over the diminished Japanese force shortly after 5 o'clock that evening. Apparently the pilots were very tired, for although the strike was very large and they concentrated on the *Ise*, they never hit her, and got only 34 near-misses.

So by late afternoon the Ozawa fleet consisted of the *Hyuga*, a light cruiser, and a destroyer heading north, followed by another light cruiser and a destroyer about 20 miles back, Off to port was the damaged light cruiser *Tama*, hit in the second attack, still streaming oil, still afloat. *Ise*, a light cruiser, and three destroyers were recovering crew survivors from the *Zuiho*. *Chiyoda* was being sunk, far to the rear, by the American cruisers that had come up to the scene. A dozen Japanese ships were still afloat.

An unprecedented sixth strike was launched by Admiral Davision's carriers that evening but accomplished nothing. The Japanese noted that after the third strike the Americans seemed to run out of gas and their following strikes were quite inept. One Japanese officer suggested that the quality of the American pilots was not very good. But that was not the answer; the quality was high and getting higher. The answer must have been fatigue, for the American carriers had been operating under extreme tension since the Taiwan air battle that began on October 10.

That night the cruisers continued the chase of the Japanese remnants. Night fighters were sent out from the carrier *Essex*. Just before darkness set in the cruisers found three destroyers and opened fire when they were 14 miles away. The destroyer *Hatsuzuki* began to run and turned to fire torpedoes. The cruiser commander, Rear Admiral L. T. Dubose, ordered the cruisers to stop and take evasive action, which they did, Twice this occurred, which slowed the pursuit, but the admiral sent three destroyers ahead to make a torpedo attack on the *Hatsuzuki*, which they did, and scored at least one hit, slowing up that big destroyer. The cruisers took the *Hatsuzuki* under fire and sank her just before 9 o'clock that night.

By that time search planes had found the Ozawa ships that remained and ascertained that even if the cruisers chased at top speed all night they could not overhaul the Japanese force until daylight, and then Ozawa would be under the protective umbrella of Japanese land-based air from Taiwan and other islands. So Admiral Dubose was told to break off the chase.

That night two American submarine wolfpacks Clarey's Crushers on the east side and Roach's Raiders on the west, closed in on the Japanese cripples. Just before sunset the submarine *Halibut* sighted the battleship *Ise*; the cruiser *Oyodo*, which was now Admiral Ozawa's flagship; and one destroyer. The *Halibut* fired six torpedoes at something that she thought was the *Ise* and five of them exploded. But the *Ise* was not sunk, nor were any of the other Japanese ships. Samuel Eliot Morison, in his history of American naval operations in World War II, suggested that they had hit a whale, or maybe a school of whales.

So that night the *Ise* and the *Hyuga* both escaped the Americans, who did not manage to come close enough to fire torpedoes. The *Tama* was not so fortunate. That crippled cruiser was trying to get home when she was found that night of October 25 by the American submarine *Jallao*, which put three torpedoes into her and sank her.

That was the end of the battle of Cape Engano, and effectively the end of the Japanese aircraft carrier force, for the *Ise* and the *Hyuga*, which had escaped the Americans here, were no more than auxiliary carriers at best, with their battleship guns and short flight decks, and in this battle they had no aircraft aboard because Admiral Ozawa put the few planes he had on the carriers that were equipped to use them best.

The battle of Cape Engano created a controversy in naval circles and among naval historians that has persisted. Admiral Kinkaid had expected Admiral Halsey to guard San Bernardino Strait against the Japanese coming through, and until the moment those pagoda masts were spotted by the sailors of Taffy Three that morning Kinkaid believed Admiral Halsey was guarding the strait. The reason for the misunderstanding is simple: Admiral Halsey reported to Admiral Nimitz in Hawaii and not to Admiral Kinkaid. Halsey was only responsible for "cooperation" with the Seventh Fleet. If he had the chance to go after the main elements of the Japanese fleet, his orders told him to do so.

Had Admiral Raymond Spruance been in command of the Third Fleet at that time he most certainly would have taken the conservative course. He was a conservative man and had thus lost the chance to destroy the Japanese fleet at the battle of the Philippine Sea. Conversely, if Spruance had been in command and had kept the Third Fleet guarding San Bernardino Strait, it is possible that they would have knocked out all the Kurita force on October 25. But they would have missed the *Zuikaku* and *Zuiho*, the only really effective carriers the Japanese had left.

What actually happened was that the escort carrier planes, which performed twice as successfully in the matter of numbers for results as did the Third Fleet aircraft, stopped Kurita with the help of the destroyers and escorts, and made him turn around and retreat, losing ships along the way.

So the net result of the battle was that the Americans sank more Japanese ships and really destroyed the Japanese navy that day. When appraising the situation, General MacArthur refused to listen to criticism of Admiral Halsey that was offered by Admiral Kinkaid and others. MacArthur said that if there was a culprit in the whole affair it had to be higher headquarters, Admiral King or the Joint Chiefs of Staff, who had permitted a divided command in the first place.

But as it eventually turned out the divided command in the Pacific did not create any real problem because the Joint Chiefs were shrewd enough to employ their forces and their leaders properly: the navy under Nimitz to carry the Pacific island campaign, which was more suitable for marine operations than the army; and then the army for the later stages of the war, when the bigger land masses of the Philippines and Okinawa were to be the scenes of battle. As for the battles of Samar and Cape Engano, it really suffices to say that the Americans won them, and that the Japanese Sho plan, developed to make utmost use of Japan's dwindling naval resources, turned out to be a total failure.

CHAPTER NINETEEN

Leyte Operations

On October 25, when it was apparent to Admiral Kinkaid that the battle for Leyte was not all over yet, he insisted that General MacArthur move ashore from the *Nashville* so the cruiser could become a part of the defense force. MacArthur again objected, so Kinkaid said he would have to move to the Barbey flagship *Wasatch* so the cruiser could be freed, and MacArthur accepted that idea. But after one night abroad the *Wasatch*, which was really an operating headquarters and not a floating hotel for generals, he decided to move ashore to the house that his staff had made ready for him. That night at dinner, when he heard grumbling from the end of the table about Admiral Halsey's "desertion" of the beachhead and the ships of the Seventh Fleet, he silenced it sharply.

In the next few days the Allies learned that the Japanese air army was not nearly so moribund as they had been led to believe. In support of the Sho Plan the Japanese Fourth Air Army had brought out all the aircraft it had denied to the navy, 2,500 planes that had been saved for army offensives and not joint operations. Early on October 26 Admiral Kinkaid asked Admiral Halsey to provide combat air patrol over Leyte Gulf. The Tacloban and Dulag airstrips had been virtually exhausted by the need to service the escort carrier planes in the battle of Samar, when those planes had shuttled back and forth from carriers to fields, and many of them had crashed in the mud of the uncompleted fields. The first of the army air force planes had not yet arrived and would not for 24 hours. Halsey was too far away to help immediately, and he really did not understand the command situation in the Philippines in which the Japanese army air forces had remained virtually intact while the navy air force, given the assignment of protecting the area from outside attack, had been decimated. If someone had told Halsey at that moment that the army air forces had 2,500 planes available for immediate operations, he would have said they were crazy.

Nor did the Japanese navy leaders in the Philippines have any idea of the army strength. They were totally concerned with their own weakness. On the night of October 25 Admiral Fukudome and Ohnishi met again at the Second Air Fleet headquarters at Clark Field. Fukudome had launched two massive conventional raids against the American naval task force, using 250 planes on each occasion, and those raids damaged two cruisers and three destroyers. It was not much of a record, Fukudome had to admit. No, said Admiral Ohnishi. His five kamikazes of the Shikishima unit had sunk one enemy carrier and damaged three.

Ohnishi was exaggerating, although he did not know it. Part of that damage done to the escort carriers had to be attributed to the army air force planes from the south, and not to the Shikishima unit. But the great difference in results was readily apparent.

After the failure of his own Second Air Fleet, Admiral Fukudome had to concede that the suicide attacks seemed the best course to pursue, given the shortage of trained pilots and the vast reservoir of dedication in the naval air establishment. So Admiral Fukudome became chief of the combined unit that was set up and Ohnishi became his chief of staff. The new unit was to be called the Combined Land-Based Air Force.

Admiral Fukudome did not intend that the whole unit would turn to kamikaze tactics, but so many of the pilots volunteered for suicide missions that he had to adjust his plans. On October 27 a total of 17 planes left Mabalacat for

Cebu, which would be the forward base of the kamikazes. That day the American carrier planes hit Manila again.

At Leyte the steel mats for the fighter strip at Tacloban arrived on October 27, and then the field that had been a sea of mud could begin to operate properly, although on a limited scale. From the beginning General Kenney was surprised and dismayed by the difference between the reality of air operations and the promise. He had expected that Admiral Halsey's carriers would supply air support until he could get the Dulag and Tacloban fields organized. But Halsey's move to Cape Engano had made it impossible for him to supply the air coverage expected. The escort carriers continued to operate.

The more important shock was to discover that although Halsey had been right about the destruction of most naval aircraft in the Philippines by the end of September, that lack did not apply to the army, which had simply concealed its planes and waited for the invasion to come. Consequently the invasion beaches from October 27 on were the scene of heavy enemy air activity that slowed Kenney's attempts to build up the Leyte air bases.

Later he complained to General Arnold, chief of the air forces, that enemy air forces should be knocked out before amphibious operations were begun. It was simply a case of not knowing the enemy well enough and not realizing that Japanese army and navy functioned as totally separate entities that had brought the invasion of Leyte so soon. Halsey had reported that Japanese air was knocked out, and indeed it was, but army air was another matter. The U.S. Fifth Air Force fighters destined for Leyte were waiting on Morotai but the engineers were delayed in getting the matting down, so the first two squadrons of P-38s did not get there until October 27. That day General MacArthur got some bad advice from his staff and declared that the army air forces were ready to assume responsibility for air cover, so Halsey began to pull his carriers out for replenishment. On October 28 came a typhoon that kept aircraft of both sides on the ground. In the next 10 days two more typhoons struck and 35 inches of rain fell on Leyte. In between storms and squalls the Americans had an unpleasant surprise. The Japanese Army Air Force resumed air activity against Fifth Air Force bases.

General Yamashita had obeyed Field Marshal Terauchi's order to make the defense of Leyte the first defense of the Philippines, although Yamashita disagreed in principle, and began almost immediately to shuttle forces into the far side of Leyte from the Manila area. For the first few days the Tenth and Twenty-fourth Corps troops made good progress although the terrain was very rugged. General Krueger had taken command of the whole Sixth Army on October 24. By October 28 the Seventeenth Infantry of the Seventh Division had reached the outskirts of the town of Dagami 10 miles inland from the Dulag invasion beaches. Here several hundred Japanese were dug in, and the Americans had to approach across a swamp before which the enemy had laid out fields of fire. The Japanese resisted every inch of the way. It was mountain terrain, slippery with rain and mud with jungle rising from swamp up the mountainside. The troops had to fight rain and mud as much as enemy troops, but by October 30 they had captured Dagami.

In the morning of October 30 the Thirty-fourth Infantry of the Twenty-fourth Division left the village of Jaro to attack the town of Carigara 20 miles northwest of the invasion beaches. Here they ran into the evidence of the new Japanese defense plan. They were stopped before they had hardly gotten out of the village. The Japanese had sent in reinforcements and had dug in on the outskirts of Jaro. The small arms fire and mortaring were intense and there were a number of American casulaties before the column pulled back. A platoon was sent forward and Colonel Red Newmans, the regimental commander, came up to see how it was going. He was wounded in the belly. He called for artillery and mortar fire. The troops hauled him back to the American line, and he survived the wound.

That night the regiment reorganized and the next morning attacked again. It was fierce fighting to drive the Japanese back toward Carigara. The artillery made the difference, By November 2 the guns were shelling Carigara and that night the troops occupied the town; the Japanese had evacuated and gone to defensive positions farther on.

On November 3 the Thirty-fourth Infantry continued its advance, west from Carigara along the coast road. The rains had stopped and the sun was shining. The Japanese coming in from Ormoc had sent a reconnaissance battalion up front and this battalion ran into the Americans. The Japanese formed a defense line behind a stream, and the Americans prepared to cross the stream and attack. Soon they did and routed the Japanese in a bloody encounter. The troops then moved toward Pinampoan. On November 4 they captured that town and Capoocan as well. Then they launched an attack southward from Carigara Bay toward Ormoc, the Japanese port of resupply, 25 miles south. The first drive was to be to Limon at the head of the Ormoc Valley. The Japanese were sending in reinforcements nearly every day to Ormoc.

General Krueger at this point was aware of the Japanese reinforcements and their intention to make the capture of Leyte expensive and slow. The Japanese could make an assault on Carigara Bay and cut off the Tenth Corps from the Twenty-fourth Corps. They had already landed the Japanese First Division at Ormoc. That division had moved into place directly south of Pinampoan, in a mountainous area, along a craggy ridge just inland from Carigara Bay, and directly in the path of the Tenth Corps. Four thousand Japanese soldiers under Lieutenant General Tadao Kataoka were dug in on the ridge.

As had now become expected, the Japanese had quickly put up a defense in depth, with mortars and artillery on the reverse slope, and on the forward slope a hive of interlocking tunnels and trenches, with timbered blockhouses, pillboxes, and firing pits established and camouflaged for automatic weapons.

As the Americans of the Twenty-fourth Infantry looked over the terrain they christened it Breakneck Ridge. That was their objective, take Breakneck Ridge and then drive on past. Major General Frederick A. Irving was in charge.

Once again the Japanese lived up to their advance billing: They fought like tigers and would not give up. The Americans had to take the ridge foot by foot, cave by cave, and trench by trench, using satchel charges, flamethrowers, and heavy artillery. The attack began on November 7 and lasted 10 days. More than 2,000 Japanese were killed.

At Tacloban, MacArthur's staff was jauntily predicting the end of the Leyte campaign before the week was out, but General Yamashita was sending more and more Japanese soldiers to Leyte to dispute the claim that victory was in sight. Meanwhile the Japanese had landed more reinforcements, the Forty-first Infantry Regiment, the Tempei Special Battalion, and the 171st Independent Infantry Battalion, who had moved into the approaches to the mountains that block the entry into Ormoc Valley.

It was obvious that the Tenth Corps did not have the strength to break through into Limon. And Japanese reinforcements continued to press into Ormoc. The Fourth Japanese Air Army sent wave after wave of fighters and bombers against the American armies. Tacloban was singled out for attack, and soon enough the Japanese airmen had found the Price house where General MacArthur had his headquarters, and it was strafed on several occasions, once while MacArthur was actually at his desk. A bullet struck the wall of his office about a foot above his head. President Osmena, who occupied quarters nearby, was also strafed repeatedly. The Japanese had control of the skies above Leyte in those first few weeks although they did not have the organization or the ability to take full advantage of it.

The Japanese attacked the airfields, and the American fighters rose to meet them, sometimes against 10:1 odds. But the fact was that the Japanese army pilots were trained almost entirely for ground support and strafing, and as air combat pilots they were far inferior to the Americans. Therefore, by November 3 the original 34 P-38s were reduced to 20 but they and the antiaircraft guns had destroyed 117 Japanese planes that week. Soon General Kenney had about 150 fighters on Leyte, but that was not enough. So he sent an SOS to Admiral Nimitz, eating his words about his ability to control the skies with land-based air. Rear Admiral Forrest Sherman came from Pearl Harbor to represent Nimitz at a meeting on November 10. MacArthur said he needed the Task Force 38 air support desperately. The task force was then at Ulithi replenishing supplies and personnel, and Admiral Halsey was planning to make a strike against Japan in November. Admiral Sherman saw that MacArthur did indeed need help against the formidable air power that had suddenly appeared in the Philippines and recommended it. Nimitz concurred, and Halsey was told that he would have to support the land operations on Leyte until November 25, a decision he took with very good grace, particularly since he still did not understand where all the new aircraft had come from.

On the ground, the Twenty-fourth Corps pushed west from its southern beachhead, not encountering any important opposition until it reached the foothills west of Dagami. As soon as it became evident that the Japanese would make a stand at Breakneck Ridge, General Krueger moved his forces to try to contain that area and pushed small units through the mountains across the neck of Leyte Island between Abuyog and Baybay. At the Camotes Sea end of the mountain road he planned a northward drive on Ormoc, perhaps supported by an amphibious landing. The Seventh Infantry Division was used for this task. It made contact with the Ninety-sixth Division on November 11 at Damulaan, 12 miles south of Ormoc. At this point a worried General Krueger was asking General MacArthur to do something about reinforcements. MacArthur, without consulting Krueger, had ordered the Seventy-seventh Infantry Division, Krueger's reserve, to go from Guam to the Solomons for a rest, rather than come to Leyte. So by early November the sixth Army was short of men—about 12,000 officers and men short—and the worst shortage was in the rifle companies, which bore the brunt of infantry action, After the Japanese landed the Twenty-sixth Infantry Division at Ormoc on November 9, Krueger played his master card, knowing how eager MacArthur was to be on to Manila. He could not move, he said, unless he had more troops. MacArthur moved fast. In a few days the Thirty-second Infantry Division and the 112th Regimental Combat Team arrived and shored up the Tenth Corps. A few days later in came the Eleventh Airborne Division, and so short of men was Krueger that he employed part of the division as regular infantry in the mountains.

They replaced the Seventh Division in the line of the Twenty-fourth Corps. Krueger was upset at the MacArthur command's moving the Seventy-seventh Division to rest and recreation when he had had a job for them to do. He wanted to make a landing near Ormoc and trap the Japanese. Now it would have to wait. He did not have the troops, and, besides, the navy fought the idea, worried still about kamikazes and air attacks, and it was tabled.

The Japanese then were almost surrounded in the narrow sector north of Ormoc. General Suzuki was held on three sides by the Americans. General Suzuki then planned an outflanking movement with two divisions that would move east from Ormoc across the mountains. General Krueger saw this threat and moved troops to a point west of Palo.

The Leyte weather alternated between bad and worse. It was the height of the Philippine typhoon season, when streams become torrents and the overcast may prevent air operations completely for days at a time.

The Americans were now getting reinforcements and new units in the line. The Thirty-second Infantry Division relieved the Twenty-fourth Division on November 16 in the Limon area. In the last week of November the Thirty-second Division and the First Cavalry Division captured Limon. By this time the Japanese First Division had suffered so much from attrition that it was no longer a strong fighting force, and by December 4, the Tenth Corps and the Twenty-fourth Corps had made contact south of Limon, and General Krueger had a solid front line in northern Leyte.

The worst American problem was supply. By this time it took three and a half days for the supplies to reach the front line from the beachheads, and that meant moving 34 tons of supplies for each regiment. Because of the mud, tracked landing craft, Buffalo, and Amphtracs tractors were used to bring the supplies up, each of them carrying four tons. Air drop was a logical solution, but not in the Philippines in the typhoon season—too many days the transports could not fly, and if they flew they could not find the ground troops.

At the end of November General Yamashita put the pressure on General Suzuki to make a drive against the Leyte airfields around Dulag and Tacloban, to stop the American air forces from cutting off the Japan air route to the Dutch East Indies.

General Suzuki then unveiled a desperate plan. He would send transport planes carrying engineer troops with demolition equipment to the major fields. They would crash-land there, immobilizing the airfield until they could destroy the facilities. A parachute drop would be made by Japanese paratroopers to support the engineers, and infantry would infiltrate through the mountains to join them. This plan was to be put in motion against the airfields at Burauen, Buri, Reyag, and San Pablo.

The attack was scheduled to begin on November 27. That day, at Tacloban, General MacArthur held a high-level planning session with his staff. The subject was the next move, which MacArthur was eager to make soon in his drive to Manila. It was the capture of Mindoro Island, which would then serve as a jump-off base for the amphibious landings on Luzon Island. Mindoro was 260 miles northwest of Leyte, and the route to reach it lay through Surigao Strait, where the Seventh Fleet had ambushed Admirals Nishimura and Shima in the early morning hours of October 25. Mindoro was important as a base for General Kenney's aircraft, which would support the Luzon landings.

All the senior commanders were there: General Kenney, General Krueger, Admiral Kinkaid, and a new one—General Eichelberger, who had been brought up from New Guinea to take command of a new army, the Eighth Army, which would shortly replace General Krueger's Sixth Army in the cleanup of the Leyte area, so General Krueger could move up to Mindoro and then to Luzon.

MacArthur, who never liked to hear opinions that strayed far from his own (unlike Admiral Nimitz, his opposite number, one of whose real strengths was his ability to give hearing to ideas very much at variance with his), was displeased almost from the beginning of the session. General Kenney spoke now of the difficulties of the Philippines weather in planning flight operations. He could not guarantee air cover of the Mindoro operation if the weather on Leyte was bad.

MacArthur then called on Admiral Kinkaid to say what the navy could do about air cover. What was to be done about Admiral Nimitz's refusal to supply warships to support the Mindoro operation? Nimitz had balked because of the heavy losses suffered by the Pacific Fleet off Leyte since the invasion. The ship losses were so great as to be extremely worrisome to the American naval high command.

After the battle of Samar, in which that first kamikaze had crashed and sunk the escort carrier *St. Lo*, the kamikaze had become more effective. On October 26, east of Surigao, three kamikazes had attacked the escort carrier *Suwannee* and damaged her. On October 27 some 15 kamikazes had attacked American ships, and one had damaged the cruiser *Denver*. On October 29 the carrier *Intrepid* had been hit, with 69 men killed, 142 wounded, and much damage done. On October 30 the kamikazes had hit the carriers *Franklin* and *Belleau Wood*. On November 1 they had hit three destroyers, the *Ammen, Anderson*, and *Claxton* in Leyte Gulf. On November 5 they had crashed the *Lexington*. On November 12 they had damaged the landing craft repair ships *Egeria* and *Achilles*, on November 17 the attack transport *Alpine*, and four days later the attack transport *James O'Hara*. On November 25, two days before MacArthur's meeting, they had attacked the carriers *Essex, Intrepid* again, *Hancock*, and *Cabot*. The *Cabot* had been hit hard, with 36 killed and 16 wounded. On the day of the meeting five kamikazes from Mabalacat had damaged the battleship *Colorado* and the cruisers *St. Louis* and *Montpelier*, and had sunk the submarine chaser *SC-744*. Small wonder, then, that Admiral Nimitz was unwilling to risk ships for a Mindoro invasion if General Kenney could not guarantee control of the air, and Kenney could not. Nimitz's attitude obviously also reflected his annoyance at having been released and called back to support the Leyte operation after MacArthur's confident statement that he did not need any more help.

MacArthur had been furious with Nimitz for refusing. Now at this meeting he learned that Kinkaid shared Nimitz's views of the coming operation. If the Mindoro operation was carried out, the ships would have to pass through Surigao Strait, and unless the army air forces could get the kamikazes under control the navy would be sitting ducks for Japanese land-based air. Kinkaid made his objections and MacArthur overruled them. Kinkaid would supply the warships, battleships, cruisers, destroyers, and escort carriers that had done so well at Samar. Actually, Kinkaid had very little faith in the escort carriers, despite their excellent record. They were too new to have yet reached the stage of endorsement by the admirals, except as ferries for aircraft to the big carrier, antisubmarine weapons for convoys (which the British had taught the Americans), and protection on the landing beaches for invasion forces after the fleet carriers had first scoured the area one or two times and then moved on.

But to escort and take responsibility for an invasion? Kinkaid did not think they were up to it. MacArthur ignored all the objections and insisted. The Mindoro invasion would go on as scheduled.

While the American generals and admirals were meeting, the proceedings were enlivened by the sounds of air battle in and around Tacloban. American antiaircraft guns began firing incessantly, and the bombs exploding and the enemy aircraft machine guns rattling threatened to disrupt the meeting, but General MacArthur feigned not to hear, and so all the others pretended not to hear, either. This was part of General Suzuki's attack plan to capture the airfields of San Pablo, Buri, and Bayug, which began that day.

It was called Operation Wa, which in Japanese means the spirit of cooperation. The plan had been developed by Lieutenant General Takaji Wachi, chief of staff of the Thirty-fifth Division.

It involved operations by several units over a period of 10 days, beginning on the night of November 27 when twin-engined transports, which looked very much like American C-47s, and in fact had been copied from the Douglas design, would land on the airstrips at Bayug and Buri. The passengers, the troops of the Kaoru Airborne Raiding Detachment, would then blow up the air facilities and aircraft and withdraw into the mountains. Then the Second Parachute Brigade would make a night paradrop and seize those two strips and San Pablo. General Suzuki would lead the attack of the Thirty-fifth Army with the 111th and Twenty-sixth divisions to link up with the paratroops, and the remnants of Sixteenth Division, which had fought at Bataan and first opposed the Leyte landings, would infiltrate from the mountains of eastern Leyte and join the coordinated assault.

The attack had begun on schedule shortly after midnight, in the early hours of November 27. The men of the Kaoru detachment had boarded four transports at Lipa, each man carrying explosives on his body. It was regarded as a highly dangerous mission and some called it suicidal. But the morale of the attackers was very high, from Lieutenant Shigeo Naka, leader of the detachment, down to the lowliest private.

Somehow in the uncertain weather the transports got lost, and although Lieutenant Naka reported by radio that they were right on schedule and on target, when the planes came down only one landed on Buri airstrip and so hard that all aboard were killed on impact. Two transports crash-landed on beaches south of Dulag, and the raiders went off into the jungle to try to find their way to the airfields. One of the planes landed in the water, and attracted the attention of an American sentry who thought the plane was a C-47 and swam out to help, to be greeted by a hail of hand grenades that made him swim back and raise the alarm. When the Japanese got ashore they were greeted with small arms fire and several of the Japanese were killed. The rest slid into the jungle.

Since the accompanying air attacks of the Fourth Air Army had caused considerable damage at Tacloban and the other airfields, the next day the American air presence was slighter than usual, which led the Japanese to believe the Naka mission had succeeded, so that night Radio Tokyo blared a strange invented story of success.

By December 1 the U.S. Sixth Army controlled most of Leyte, except the San Isidro Peninsula west of Carigara Bay and a half-moon sector about 12 miles in radius west of Ormoc. Here the Japanese had 35,000 men, but the Sixth Army now numbered 183,000. Some 24,000 Japanese had been killed in the hard fighting to this date, and the Americans had suffered casualties of 2,260 killed and missing and about 8,000 sick and wounded. Dysentery, heat rash, fungus infections, immersion foot, and all the other troubles of the jungle caused almost as much trouble as the enemy.

On that day, December 1, General MacArthur came closer to being killed than at any other time, and by Americans. He was working in his office in Price house when an air raid began and the antiaircraft guns started to bark. A shell from an antiaircraft gun punched through the bedroom wall and came to rest on the office couch. It did not explode. The general picked up the projectile later and presented it to the officer in charge of antiaircraft with the suggestion that they raise their sights.

The Japanese were anything but finished, no matter how it looked. At the San Pablo Airfield the operations officer of the Eleventh Airborne Division received that day what was called "a crystal ball report," which was really a report based on the code-breaking pioneered by the navy. He took the report to Major General Joseph Swing, the commander of the airborne division. It said that the Japanese were planning an airborne attack against the three airfields they wanted to capture. General Swing laughed at the report. There was not much he could do about it anyhow at the moment because his Eleventh Airborne troops were fighting as infantry in the Mahonag Mountains, far to the west, or guarding Twenty-fourth Corps dumps on the landing beaches.

Nobody expected much more trouble. The intelligence officer of the Twenty-fourth Corps on the night of December 4 noted in his daily intelligence analysis that organized resistance on Leyte was almost over. But the Japanese did not know about that report, and on December 5 they began the second stage of their attempt to take over the airfields. Soldiers of the Sixteenth Division slipped down from the mountain passes to the Buri airstrip and attacked. The troops they faced were headquarters troops, signal troops, and engineers.

Security was very lax and most of the men were sleeping just before dawn on December 6 when the Japanese attacked the barracks area, bayoneting, grenading, and shooting men in their sleeping bags. The Japanese hit battalion headquarters where nine engineer officers were sleeping and shot all of them before they could get out of their hammocks.

Some of the construction men fought back with what weapons they had, but in short order the Japanese had control of the field and the Americans had disappeared into the jungle.

So the enemy had succeeded at Buri. That same day 1,400 Japanese paratroops of the Second Parachute Brigade prepared for their assault on the American airfields. Since there was a shortage of transport planes, only half the troops would land the first day; the other half would come in the following day.

Lieutenant Colonel Tsunehiro Shirai led the Third Parachute Regiment, which would jump in three waves, again an unwelcome improvisation made necessary by the shortage of aircraft.

This was a crack outfit, Many of the officers spoke English, which they intended to use to confuse the Americans. They planned to come in at dusk, knowing that their transports looked very much like C-47s.

The first wave loaded up in 26 transports, and by 3:40 P.M. they were on their way from Lipa and Angeles airfields. Most of the paratroops were scheduled to drop on Buri and the rest on San Pablo Airfield and Bayag. At twilight the planes were over San Pablo and were observed by General Swing and some other officers, who wondered what this flight of C-47s was doing coming in at this time, The planes dropped to 700 feet, and then one officer noticed that the plane interior lights were on and there was a man standing in the open doorway of each plane. As airborne troops they knew what this meant, although they found it hard to believe it was happening to them. When the planes were over the airfield bodies came tumbling out, and the men of the Eleventh Airborne who had been standing in the chow line suddenly forgot about eating and dashed for their tents to get their weapons.

The Japanese landed right on top of the division command post and started by burning and wrecking the planes on the strip. At one end of San Pablo a number of Eleventh Airborne troops had been packing bundles to drop for their comrades in the Mahonag Mountains when they saw the Japanese descending. They broke open the bundles and retrieved the packed weapons and set up a perimeter. Just after darkness came, they saw a column of men, rifles slung, marching toward them singing "Sweet Adeline." Lieutenant David Carnahan set up behind a machine gun. He was in charge of the group of about 40 Americans. He did not doubt that the newcomers were Eleventh Airborne, but what the hell were they doing all that singing for?

Then the column stopped about 20 yards away and the leader moved up, aimed a flashlight at the Americans, and asked:

"Is this the machine gun at the east end of the airstrip?"

There was something wrong with the accent.

"Yes, sir," Carnahan replied, and squeezed the trigger of the machine gun. The Japanese officer fell, still cluching his flashlight, and so did several others. The rest disappeared into the darkness.

Most of the Japanese had dropped on San Pablo, and only about 50 of them parachuted into Buri airstrip, including Colonel Shirai. The second wave was already on its way at Lipa airfield on Luzon, but it was caught in the weather, and after flying a very short distance had to return to base. The third wave of the night did not get off at all. So Colonel Shirai and a handful of men were trying to take Buri and the rest of the first wave was fighting on San Pablo. There the confusion was enormous. In the darkness men could not tell friend from foe and Japanese and Americans were separated into small groups. One American officer leaped into a two-man foxhole to escape a burst of fire. The foxhole was already occupied. He was there until dawn when he suddenly realized that his companion was a Japanese. The Japanese hit him twice with his bayonet, and then the officer fired his carbine and hit the Japanese in the head.

General Swing organized a detachment of clerks and other headquarters personnel to set up some sort of defense and they began chasing the Japanese off their airfield. But the Japanese moved into the jungle and to Buri to join Lieutenant Colonel Shirai and the troops of the Sixteenth Division.

Now the 187th Glider Battalion launched an attack on Buri. At about noon on December 7 infantrymen of the American Twenty-eighth Division arrived at San Pablo a battalion strong, and General Swing sent them to join the fight to regain Buri. The infantrymen had to work their way through deep swamp. When they arrived at Buri, they found the Japanese in control and dug in. The Japanese 111th and Twenty-sixth divisions were to have come up by this time to link up with the paratroops, and had they arrived it might have been a different story. But the Japanese got bogged down in the mountains in the west by slippery mud and deep jungle and were slowed by fighting with elements of the Eleventh Airborne Division in the Mahonag Mountains. So they did not arrive at all, and the Japanese paratroops and Sixteenth Division troops were left to try to hold alone. They stopped the Americans at first with machine gun fire. But eventually the Americans moved four battalions into Buri and fought the Japanese for three days. On December 10 they made a final assault and recaptured the field. The Japanese then moved down the road to Bureuen, where the Fifth Air Force had its headquarters, and shot up the headquarters building and other installations, but theirs was a hopeless task. Deep in the heart of American territory and outnumbered, they had no chance of making a success of Operation Wa.

On December 1 General Krueger dusted off his plan for the pincers movement around Ormoc to be carried out by an amphibious landing of the Seventy-seventh Division. This time he was successful and the objections of the navy were overcome. One reason for that was the betterment of land-based air operations. At the end of November, when the carriers were again eager to be off on more exciting business, General MacArthur admitted that General Kenney still did not have air matters under control and asked for several squadrons of marine night fighters from the Palaus and the Solomons. Since Nimitz was very much concerned about kamikaze operations, he agreed and the fighters began arriving at Tacloban on December 3. For the next month the marines defended the area against night raiders.

The extent of the Americans' underestimation of the Japanese air strength in the Philippines became apparent at the end of the Leyte campaign. Between October 20 and the end of the year planes and antiaircraft guns shot down nearly 1,500 Japanese planes.

This time the navy reluctantly agreed to the Ormoc operation. General MacArthur had hoped to move faster but the slowness of movement on Leyte had made him postpone the Mindoro operation for 10 days. Instead they would undertake Kreuger's Ormoc landing. The reason was simply the need to wipe out the Japanese enclave.

Almost a month earlier Krueger and MacArthur had discussed the problems of the battle and the reasons for slow progress: weather and lack of replacements. But help was coming. Major General William Gill's Thirty-second Division, a veteran of the New Guinea wars, arrived on November 14 and relieved the exhausted Twenty-fourth Division in the line at Breakneck Ridge. Gill soon sent two regiments around the Japanese left flank and a third around Breakneck Ridge. On November 22 Limon was captured, and soon the Americans were astride Highway 2, two miles south of Limon, leaving enemy pockets behind in the Breakneck Ridge area, but taking the gateway from the north to the Ormoc Valley. It had been an expensive campaign, with 700 Americans killed.

So the stage was set for Krueger's amphibious operation and Major General Andrew D. Bruce's Seventy-seventh Division was available, as were the naval vessels needed. Also, as noted, the air situation had improved considerably in recent days.

Still, all of Task Group Commander Rear Admiral Arthur Struble's caveats were realized in the amphibious operation.

The first move was the delivery of some troops on the west coast inside the American lines, necessary because of the bad condition of the roads. This task group left Leyte Gulf on December 4 and came under attack although the mission was successfully accomplished. But when the returning convoy was in the Surigao Strait, it was attacked by a number of kamikazes. The army P-38s, which were flying combat air patrol, shot down several, and so did the ships' antiaircraft guns. But one kamikaze crashed the deck of *LSM-20*, killing eight men, wounding nine, and sinking the vessel. Another kamikaze hit the water alongside *LM-23* and ricocheted into her, causing much damage. A third one into the destroyer *Drayton* killed six men and wounded 12.

Later in the day, off the Cabugan Islands, an army bomber attacked the destroyer *Mugford* and dropped a bomb that missed. But the pilot seemed to have been wounded and decided to crash the plane into the ship: He did and two men were killed and six burned so severely that they died later.

Two days later came the Ormoc landings. The ships arrived three miles south of Ormoc off the beach, in the early hours of December 7. At 6:38 the destroyers began a shore bombardment and rocket-equipped landing craft blasted the 1,200-yard landing beach with rockets. At 7:07 the troops landed on the beach without a single casualty. The future looked very bright. That day word came of a Japanese convoy heading to the northwest. Army air force planes were sent out, but the convoy had landed 4,000 fresh troops for the Japanese.

On the beach at Ormoc everything was going very well that morning. General Bruce assumed command of the troops ashore at 9:30 in the morning, and they soon realized that they had surprised the enemy and the going initially would be easy. But at 9:34 bogeys began to appear on the radar screens of the ships.

Attack was by army air force planes on the destroyers *Ward* and *Mahan*, and the minesweepers *Sumter* and *Scout*, which were on antisubmarine patrol. The first formation consisted of bombers protected by fighters. Above them the U.S. P-38s swooped down and hit three fighters and two bombers, and when they were hit turned to dive on the ships. One hit the *Mahan* abaft the bridge, and within seconds she was hit by two other bombers turned kamikaze. The *Mahan* had to slow to keep the fires from being fanned, and soon the fires spread so that they could not be controlled and the men abandoned ship, with 10 killed and 32 wounded. The *Mahan* was then sunk by gunfire from the destroyer *Walke*.

As Admiral Struble had feared, the Fifth Air Force was still underestimating the power of the Japanese air forces.

The Americans found it hard to differentiate, but they were being hit by Japanese army air force planes and navy planes. The difference was that the navy planes had now all become kamikazes, under the agreement between Admiral Fukudome and Admiral Ohnishi. The army planes were still using traditional tactics, although the air of change was blowing in Tokyo in the army, too.

The next casualty to the ships that day was the old destroyer *Ward*, which was hit by three kamikazes. The first hit just above the waterline and created an enormous explosion that started fires, then two other suicide divers crashed her and she became a piece of wreckage. The crew abandoned ship, and the *Ward* was sunk by the destroyer *O'Brien*.

For the next hour there were no attacks. Admiral Struble got ready for the return trip to Leyte. But on the way, the Japanese attackers came again, kamikazes and conventional. One crashed into the destroyer *Liddle*, hitting the flying bridge and killing her captain and wounding several other officers. In all, she lost 36 killed and missing, and 22 wounded.

At about 1:30 that afternoon, the destroyer *Edwards* was attacked as she was taking wounded off the *Liddle*. The plane was an army twin-engine reconnaissance plane and it dropped a large bomb that narrowly missed the destroyer. Almost immediately the *Edwards* was also attacked by more army planes, bombing and strafing, and a kamikaze sneaked in with them and crashed into the destroyer *Lamson* amidships, killing 231 men and wounding 50. The ship was saved, however.

At this time more kamikazes attacked the destroyer *Barton* but did not connect, and later in the day as the ships steamed toward Leyte Gulf they came under attack again, but the Japanese did not connect.

Before the day was out the Japanese had made 16 separate large-scale raids on the Struble force and had damaged five of his ships badly.

Now that the Seventy-seventh Division had been landed at Ormoc, it had to be supplied. And as experience on Leyte had showed, the weather and the roads were unreliable and the best method of supply for Ormoc was the sea.

The Japanese knew that, too. On the day the Americans landed at Ormoc, a reinforced infantry regiment, an artillery battalion, and a special naval landing force landed north of Ormoc to reinforce the Japanese army. The convoy was bombed by American army air force planes and the landing was so disturbed that only 400 troops landed in the Ormoc area and the rest moved north to the San Isidro Peninsula, which put them up with the isolated northern force.

On December 8 both the Japanese army air force planes and the navy kamikazes seemed to have taken the day off. That was the day Admiral Struble sent the first resupply convoy to Ormoc. December 9 was also quiet, but December 10 arrived and with it the Japanese air forces. Leyte Gulf was hit again, and a kamikaze dived into the destroyer *Hughes*. The Liberty ship *William S. Ladd* took another kamikaze that caused much damage, completely wrecking the small craft.

On December 11 the American air forces attacked a Japanese convoy bound for the back side of Leyte, sank three transports, and cost the Japanese a whole battalion of troops. But the Japanese still managed to reinforce Leyte with others in the same convoy.

On December 11 at 9:30 in the morning the second Ormoc resupply convoy left Leyte Gulf—eight landing ships medium and four LCIs, with an escort of six destroyers. They had only four fighter planes for air cover.

At about 5 o'clock that evening the convoy was heading at 12 knots toward Ormoc when a group of kamikazes came in to attack. Four of them concentrated on the destroyer *Reid*. Three of the four connected, and the *Reid* sank in two minutes. Japanese planes then strafed the survivors who were struggling in the water until marine Corsairs drove them away. Only about half of the *Reid*'s crew of 300 men survived.

The destroyer *Caldwell* was next on the Japanese list. She knocked down one kamikaze that was just about to crash the ship. More kamikazes attacked but were driven off. By darkness the convoy was safe for the night.

On December 12 the destroyer *Caldwell* caught a kamikaze, one of three that made a concerted attack on her. One wing hit the ship's bridge, and the damage was severe. Simultaneously the ship came under attack from conventional army planes bombing. The damage control parties of the ship were very efficient and in an hour she was working again and the fires were out.

It was obvious that the kamikazes represented quite a formidable obstacle, and as the year ended, the army air forces got on the kamikaze bandwagon. They were losing many planes in the Philippines, their pilots obviously were not equal to the new breed of American aviators, and their aircraft were mostly inferior to the new American designs. So the army began to adopt suicide tactics as well, and the problem continued to grow for the American navy.

It was a very serious matter indeed, and shortly one of the few censoring actions of the war would take place at high levels. Admiral Nimitz, with General MacArthur concurring, would order a news blackout on the kamikaze attacks so that the Japanese would not learn how much damage they were doing and how worried the naval high command was becoming. In fact, soon Admiral King would create a special naval section in Boston that would do nothing but study methods of dealing with the kamikazes. No solution was ever found other than that advocated by Admiral Halsey: to hit them first, and when they got into the air, to attack them relentlessly with aircraft and antiaircraft. It was certainly no complete solution, but the fact was that there could be no complete solution to a situation in which a young man was willing to give his life for a chance to put a bomb into a warship.

After landing, the Seventy-seventh Infantry Division moved inland quickly, taking advantage of the surprise they had created within the Japanese command. Three days later they captured Ormoc, and then it was impossible for General Yamashita to reinforce his troops on Leyte. Nor could they be supplied except by barge along deserted sectors of the coastline. But General Suzuki had no intention of surrendering. He led his troops into the mountains and continued to fight.

While the Seventy-seventh Division moved toward Ormoc, the 511th Parachute Infantry Regiment of the Eleventh Airborne Division moved out of the Mahonag Mountains east of Ormoc in an attack toward the west coast.

The Japanese were not beaten but they were contained. General MacArthur announced that the Ormoc operations had split the enemy forces into two parts, isolating those in the north from those along the coast in the south, and that it should not be long before enemy activity on Leyte ceased. That was an overoptimistic statement, but the real danger was finished. The Japanese could fight and die—and they did—but they could no longer influence the course of events. General Suzuki asked General Yamashita to change the mission of the Thirty-fifth Army to one of strategic delay. Two more convoys would make it to western Leyte successfully, but that was all, for General Yamashita announced to Suzuki that thereafter the Thirty-fifth Army was on its own. No more help would be coming from Manila.

So after Ormoc, MacArthur was free to go on toward Manila. By the end of the year MacArthur announced that the Leyte campaign had been reduced to mopping-up operations. General Eichelberger's Eighth Army took over these operations, which lasted until May 1945.

CHAPTER TWENTY

Mindoro

As the battle for Leyte continued, more and more General MacArthur's thoughts were focused on the coming move to Luzon, where he expected to fight the final battle of the Philippines—not on Leyte, as Field Marshal Terauchi would have it. But for the Luzon invasion the land based air forces would have to take over. They had been very slow to move into Leyte. The terrain was terrible, the heavy clay did not drain properly, and pools of water formed in every depression with every rain. There was no way to make that Leyte airfield much better than seas of mud; even Marston matting did not solve the problem because there were aprons and grass where the Marston matting was not laid down, and they were always treacherous.

For the invasion of Luzon, MacArthur needed air superiority, and as the Leyte invasion continued and the number of kamikazes and conventional attack planes far exceeded the expectations of the Allies, it became more important that these telling attacks be contained. By November the kamikaze damage to navy ships had become the navy's most serious problem and one to which no one had any solution except to keep the damage to a minimum. Therefore, when General MacArthur said he wanted to establish a base at Mindoro, 300 miles north of Leyte, the navy jibbed. Admiral Kinkaid spoke for the navy then, saying that the Mindoro invasion would be very costly in terms of ships and lives, and opposed it as too dangerous to warrant the cost. But MacArthur had no reasonable alternative, and neither did anyone else. The real problem with Mindoro was that it was ringed by other islands with enemy air bases. The great advantage of Mindoro is that it was lightly defended (about a thousand men) and had four airfields.

On November 15 the MacArthur plan called for the invasion of Luzon on December 20, with the invasion of Mindoro on December 5, after which the air force engineers and construction men would work frantically to get those airfields ready in time. This was essential to the suppression of the kamikaze attacks. But on November 15, when Admiral Kinkaid arrived at Tacloban for a check with General MacArthur, he found that the kamikaze problem was perhaps worse than ever. Just about everybody at MacArthur's headquarters agreed that the Mindoro operation ought to be delayed until air control could be established and that the Lingayen Gulf landings should similarly be delayed.

The only one who really disagreed was General MacArthur, to whom postponement of the operation against Luzon was pure torture. On November 16 MacArthur sent a long dispatch to Admiral Nimitz justifying his plans, and he called for the return of the Third Fleet to the Philippines, because he admitted that General Kenney's land-based air forces were unable to provide the air cover needed.

But Nimitz had problems of his own. The Third Fleet task groups all needed replenishment and they had to have two weeks. He could maintain air cover until November 26, but by then he had to do something for the carriers.

On November 17 General Kenney's staff announced that if the navy could cover Leyte and and protect the Mindoro convoy on its first day out, then Kenney's planes could cover the rest of the operation. But there was a caveat, the navy had to base 12 squadrons ashore for 10 days, and there was no place to base them.

Also at this time Rear Admiral Arthur D. Struble told Kinkaid that the Mindoro operation threatened to be deadly to American naval vessels. The Japanese were aware of the coming movement and could bring forces onto all the neighboring islands and use them as bases for attack on Mindoro. And General Kenney told him that there was not enough space for the 12 squadrons of navy and marine planes that had been offered the Southwest Pacific Command for the Mindoro operation.

The problem of the kamikazes was underlined on November 25 when they came down like hail on the Third Fleet carriers and damaged four of the nine fast carriers involved there. Next day Halsey had had enough. He canceled the remaining strikes and sent three of the four task groups to Ulithi.

That same day MacArthur called a meeting to make final plans for the assault on Mindoro; he planned to go in on December 5. General Kenney said he could handle the air protection with his land-based airplanes. General Krueger said the troops were ready. Kinkaid and his staff painted a very grim picture, guessing that they would lose 25 percent of their ships, and he could not accept such casualties and still take General MacArthur's armies to Luzon in a few more weeks. But he could put together a force of six escort carriers, three battleships, three light cruisers, and 18 destroyers for the Mindoro landings. But the navy men continued to be troubled and on November 29, three days before the Mindoro expedition was scheduled to depart from Leyte, Admiral Struble suggested that the whole plan be tabled. There had been more kamikaze attacks on big ships in Leyte Gulf. Kinkaid's subordinates were almost uniformly against the project, but Kinkaid knew that MacArthur's heart was set on it.

The controversy came to a head on November 30 in two meetings between MacArthur and Kinkaid. MacArthur insisted that Japanese air power had vanished. Kinkaid knew better, but MacArthur refused to budge. He would have his way. Kinkaid went back to his command ship to send a message to Admiral King that would have caused King to forbid the mission, and then the quarrel between army and navy would have broken into the open. But an alternative plan was offered—a delay would permit the fast carriers to replenish and rest and then they would support the operation. MacArthur did not like it but finally agreed to delay the Mindoro operation for 10 days and the Lingayen operation for 20 days.

The Mindoro invasion force left the east coast of Leyte on December 12, traveling through the Mindanao Sea.

General MacArthur had another close call with death or injury that he did not even know about. He had wanted to go along on this invasion trip and ride in the flagship *Nashville*, but at the last moment he was persuaded by his staff not to go.

On December 13 they were off the southern trip of Negros Island and about to enter the Sulu Sea when a flock of kamikazes, flying low under the radar net, suddenly appeared and attacked. One crashed into the *Nashville*, killing 133 people, wounding 199 others, and virtually disrupting the landing troop organizations. Many of those affected had been on the bridge, where MacArthur would certainly have been had he made the trip. The dead men included the chiefs of staff of Admiral Struble's force and of General William Dunckel's landing force, and Dunckel himself was wounded. The command was tranferred to a destroyer. Two hours later a kamikaze crashed into a destroyer, causing 40 more casualties. Next day the Japanese sent down a huge force of 186 planes, which fortunately missed the convoy.

So the landing force went ashore on Mindoro on December 15 without incident or opposition until they got inland, for there were only 1,000 Japanese troops on the entire island.

But in spite of all the air cover afforded by the P-38s and carrier aircraft, a number of kamikazes broke through the screen that day and crashed into three landing ships, two destroyers, and escort carriers that day. For the next few weeks Admiral Struble's resupply convoys were regularly attacked as he said they would be.

As one navy spokesman put it, it was hard all the way. Never since the Anzio landing in Italy had the American navy had so much trouble supporting a military operation.

By Christmas the Fifth Air Force was operating from two San Jose airfields and a third was almost ready. These fields made all the difference, and they were necessary because on December 19 the Third Fleet was hit by a typhoon that sank three destroyers, damaged seven other ships, and cost the force 186 lost carrier planes. Halsey had to take the fleet to Ulithi for repairs and replenishment.

On the day after Christmas a force of Japanese cruisers and destroyers attacked the Mindoro beachhead but the ships were driven off by a fierce assault by PT boats and the planes of the Fifth Air Force. They sank a Japanese destroyer and damaged several other ships.

On January 1 control of the Mindoro activity passed from General Krueger to General Eichelberger's Eighth Army, and for the rest of that month a number of landings were conducted at various points on the island in the mopping-up operations. Mindoro was very definitely under control, and as far as the Luzon landings were concerned it had proved to be a wise precaution by General MacArthur, even though the cost in ships and men was high. Without Mindoro the first days on Luzon might have been very different; the fighting on Mindoro had cost the Japanese heavily in terms of air power. They lost about a hundred planes on Mindoro from kamikaze and conventional attacks. By the time the Americans were ready to go into Lingayen the Fifth Air Force had put three fighter groups, two medium bomber groups, and seven miscellaneous squadrons on this island. Just then it would provide air cover for the Lingayen landings. But after that it would be equally valuable, providing air cover for operations in the central and southern Philippines.

It was apparent at the time of the Luzon attack that had the Allies not held Mindoro, MacArthur would not have been able to move to Luzon when he did.

CHAPTER TWENTY-ONE

The Rush to Manila

By the time that General MacArthur got ready to invade Luzon, the Mindoro base had become very strong and very important to the program. Here was the air support he needed; it was a long time in coming but it had come in time.

For months MacArthur had been planning this invasion of Luzon. He had considered at least 10 different "Mike" plans, which meant Luzon, but always came back to the time-honored plan that General Homma had used in his invasion of the Philippines four years earlier because it was the simplest and the best. The place to go was Lingayen Gulf: It had the best beaches, it had the shortest and straightest route to Manila, and the countryside lent itself to armored operations because it was level.

Three weeks later secondary landings would be made northwest of Bataan and 20 miles south of Corregidor.

Admiral Kinkaid was responsible for getting the troops there. The Third Fleet would come in to cover the landings, with its four air task groups of Admiral Halsey and Admiral Mitscher's Task Force 38. General Kenney's air force would provide air support and this time it would be effective air support. After the troops of the First Corps and Twenty-fourth Corps were safely ashore the land commanders would take over, and they would drive to Manila.

General MacArthur's intelligence section estimated that General Yamashita had 152,000 troops on Luzon—a rash underestimate because he had far closer to 250,000. General Krueger's Sixth Army numbered 203,000, but only 131,000 were combat troops. With other forces and the guerrillas who were now being enlisted in an organized fashion the Allied army came to 280,000, which made it by far the biggest military operation yet staged in the Pacific. And the tactics for this operation would be army tactics, employing the full range of army weapons, tanks, and artillery especially, in a manner that had not been done before.

It was an enormously complicated operation, involving troops from Leyte, but also troops from nine other bases as far away as Hollandia, Noumea, and Bougainville. Later the force would be augmented by another corps, the Eleventh Corps, and part of the Eighth Army, including the Eleventh Airborne Division. The Eleventh Corps would seal off Bataan, and the Eleventh Airborne would advance on Manila from the south, thus providing one arm of the pincers movement with the Sixth Army's approach from the northwest on Manila.

For the first eight days of January the Americans had planned a major air operation and it came off, with navy, army, and marine corps planes striking Japanese airfields and shipping all during the daylight and some of the nighttime hours. The airmen, as usual, came back with glowing reports of destruction but now MacArthur's commanders were battlewise and they sensed that somewhere the Japanese were saving a Sunday punch, that their kamikazes would appear in force at some point during the early operations. So they made themselves as ready as they could be.

General MacArthur was determined to accompany the task force. He would board the cruiser *Boise* on January 4, and many of his staff would go with him because he intended to set up headquarters on Luzon as quickly as possible and encourage speed in the drive on Manila.

In the nights before the invasion was to get going the lights burned long at headquarters. There were many worried men. The assault convoy would have to wend its way through narrow seas, between islands held by the enemy, up the China Sea, past Manila, looping around Bataan and Corregidor, all fortified places where the Japanese might try to stop them from the sea and in the air. Many of the soldiers made their wills, not because they expected to die, but one never knew.

And so the convoy assembled, 160 battleships and lesser ships of Admiral Oldendorf's support group, destroyers, minesweepers, and escort carriers. They steamed through the Sulu Sea on January 4 ahead of the main convoy, and kamikazes attacked. They sank the escort carrier *Ommaney Bay* that day, and the next day off Bataan they crashed into two cruisers, another escort carrier, a destroyer escort, and a landing craft.

The support group reached Lingayen Gulf on January 6 and began the bombardment, and the kamikazes came again. The battleship *New Mexico* was hit, killing the British liaison officer, who was a good friend to MacArthur. But all this carnage had one good element: By the time the troop transports arrived in the wake of the support force, the kamikazes had shot their wad and so the attacks were not as severe as some had expected. And yet Admiral Barbey's landing force, of which the *Boise* was a part, came under attack off Mindoro on January 7, and the *Boise* was almost hit by a bomb. They had something new, too. General MacArthur watched two torpedoes come at the *Boise* and miss because of the skill of those on the bridge, and then he watched the midget submarine surface and be rammed by a destroyer. MacArthur was living up to his reputation for managing somehow to get into the thick of the action as no other major commander ever did.

The next day as the convoy steamed off Corregidor, General MacArthur stood on the bridge, watching the skyline, deep in thought. They were again attacked by kamikazes but no damage was done to the *Boise*.

On January 9 as the sun rose over Lingayen Gulf a thousand ships lay off the southern shore. During the preassault bombardment the kamikazes came again, but in diminished numbers. The Japanese naval command had exhausted its resources, and the army wasn't far behind, having now decided that they too must go the kamikaze route. A battleship, two cruisers, a destroyer escort, and the cruiser *Australia* of the Australian navy were hit, the *Australia* for the fifth time since leaving Leyte Gulf.

The landings were very easy. There was no opposition because General Yamashita had opted to use three defense lines. One line would start in the mountains of Lingayen and would cover the coastal plain. Another line, manned by a second group, would defend Manila, and the third defense line, commanded by General Yamashita, would move to Baguio in the mountains and continue the battle from there. Yamashita's defenses did not anticipate winning any major battles or driving the Americans away. It was too late for that; he did plan to make victory very costly and the process as long as possible, thus tying up thousands of troops, many aircraft, and many ships, and in that way delaying the assault of the enemy on the Japanese homeland. This was the best that Yamashita could do and he turned to the task grimly, determined to fight until the bitter end.

Only the Forty-third Division, which seized San Fabian and drove beyond, began to find serious opposition as it moved into the mountain area. This worried General Krueger, who was really expecting a strong counterattack at some point from Yamashita, but did not know when and how it would come.

At 2 P.M. on invasion day, General MacArthur went ashore on Lingayen. This time, unlike the Leyte landing, the coming ashore was staged for effect. MacArthur insisted on getting his feet wet although there was no need for it. But the actor in MacArthur emerged again and he played the landing for the crowds of Filipinos and the Americans back home for all it was worth.

After landing MacArthur wandered up and down the beach chatting with Filipinos who had come to see him land and officers and men who were busy unloading supplies on the beach. Later he visited Sixteenth Division headquarters and then got into a jeep and started for Dagupan, the provincial capital, where he intended to make his initial field headquarters. But the bridges were washed out by bombing and he could not get there that day, so he came back to spend the night on the *Boise*.

That night the Japanese had a new surprise for the Americans. They sent 70 suicide boats, motorboats laden with high explosives, against the invasion fleet. And they managed to ram two landing craft and four LSTs, but that was all. Most of the suicide boats were sunk by gunfire from the destroyers and escorts and the lesser vessels, and the survivors went back to reorganize and prepared to try again.

On January 10 MacArthur went ashore again and made an inspection of every one of the four divisional sectors of the invasion front. He stayed aboard the *Boise* on the 11th and 12th, but on the 13th he moved into the government buildings at Dagupan. By that time the Lingayen airfield had been prepared to handle fighters, but the kamikaze threat was gone. A new estimate put the total number of Japanese aircraft left at about a dozen. The Japanese air forces had tried their best but had failed again.

By January 17 the Fourteenth Corps was 27 miles from the Lingayen beach and only 35 miles north of Clark Field, the big aero complex which had been the center of American air activity before 1942. MacArthur was eager to be off and impatient with delay that kept him out of Manila, for which he expected no fight. He believed that Yamashita would do what he had done four years earlier, declare it an open city to prevent the destruction of the city and the effect on the people. To encourage this he wanted General Krueger to hurry.

On January 17 an impatient MacArthur told Krueger the drive must be hurried up, he wanted them to get to Clark Field and the low casualty rate indicated that it could be done faster. Krueger, still worried about his exposed flank and the big Japanese army that had not come forth, did not hurry fast enough, so on January 25 MacArthur moved his headquarters inland to Hacienda Luisita, which was out ahead of Krueger's headquarters and had to be an embarassment to the general. MacArthur was very impatient by this time and his staff, as always, reflected the general's wishes. So the talk went around that Krueger was too cautious and ought to be sent home. Eichelberger, who ranked second to Krueger, was the loudest in the complaint.

At this point the Americans were up against Major General Rikichi Tsukada's Kembu Group, 30,000 troops charged with the defense of Clark Field. They were to fight and then withdraw into the Zambales Mountains and fight some more, delaying tactics.

Ahead of them in Manila, Lieutenant General Shizuo Yokoyama's Shimbu Group of 80,000 was to do what MacArthur expected: abandon the city and move into the mountains. But first they were to move thousands of tons of supplies up to the Baguio area that Yamashita had chosen for his central defensive position. A part of this group was the navy contingent commanded by Rear Admiral Sanji Iwabuchi, 20,000 sailors who were to obey the general's orders.

Yasmashita, with 152,000 men, was going to fight to the end between Baguio, Bambang, and Bontok.

On January 28 there was some hard fighting of the Twenty-fifth Division troops at Binalonan and San Manuel. MacArthur was visiting that sector at the time and saw the American line reeling as the Japanese attacked with tanks. He hastened to the area of the 161st Infantry and in the fashion for which he was known engaged in the war at the level of a combat infantry commander, helping Colonel James Dalton II rally the troops and fight off the Japanese attack.

They were coming close to old stamping grounds now. The Sixth Division secured the Cabaruan Hills and then drove nearly to Cabanatuan. The Sixth Ranger Battalion's Company C and part of Company F were designated to make a raid and rescue the prisoners. They had been informed by guerrillas about the camp and the Japanese guards, about 300 in number.

On the 29th the Rangers made their bivouac about a mile from the prison camp. The guerrillas would go along the main road northeast of the camp and forestall any action by a garrison of about 800 Japanese there. The Company F platoon would steal in the back door of the camp and kill the guards there. When they opened fire the main body of Rangers would assault the front gate. Everything was laid out. They knew where the Japanese kept their vehicles, where they slept, and where the prisoners were kept. The guerrillas had spotted it all for them. They knew where the telephone lines ran so they could cut them.

And so the Rangers and the guerrillas went into action. Just after 6 P.M. they converged on the prison camp. From the back and front of the camp the firing began and Japanese guards started to fall. With grenades, bazookas, rifles, and knives they assaulted the Japanese. Four trucks in the tin shed where trucks were kept had been loaded up with Japanese soldiers a few minutes before the Rangers struck, and when they poured bazooka fire into the shed, they eliminated many guards, too.

The Rangers wanted the POWs to move out fast but they could not; they had no will to resist and very little strength. Meanwhile a Japanese force in the south led by a tank was trying to break through to the prison camp. But by 10:30 that night the Rangers had rescued 531 men, missing only one frightened man who hid under his bunk, and the column began to withdraw. They marched all night through Japanese-held territory, with the Japanese column chasing and not far behind. They were given food and water as they passed through Filipino villages or barrios. At 11 o'clock the next day they made contact with a convoy of trucks and ambulances that had been sent to rescue them, and they met at the barrio of Sibul and soon pulled out to safety.

A Ranger unit made a raid on the prison camp there. Four months earlier the inmates of this POW camp had begun to see American planes over Luzon as Admiral Halsey's carriers blasted the Japanese airfields. Since that time they had been waiting for liberation, 500 of them, the remnants of the "Battling Bastards of Bataan." Originally the prisoners had numbered 7,000 penned up at Cabanatuan, but some had been shipped to Taiwan, some to Manchuria, some to Japan. In December 1944 more were transferred to Old Bilibid Prison in Manila. Over the three years hundreds of the inmates of Cabanatuan had died from sickness and mistreatment.

Meanwhile the Sixth Division overran San Jose, but most of the Japanese got through to the mountains of the north. The Americans did destroy most of the Japanese Sixth Tank Division, which was Yamashita's most important armored unit.

About two miles north of Clark Field the Japanese began to offer serious resistance on January 23, but by January 28 the Fortieth Division had captured that complex of airfields called Clark Field. On the 30th MacArthur made a trip by jeep to Clark Field, even though the fighting was still going on there and shells came in frequently. That day he sent a strong message to Krueger demanding faster action. On the 31st the Thirty-seventh Division seized Calumpit, which is only 25 miles northwest of Manila.

The Eleventh Corps had landed on the coast northwest of Bataan and set out to seal off Bataan. They ran into strong Japanese defense eastward in the mountain area near Olangapo. Then on January 31 the Eleventh Airborne landed south of Corregidor and moved down Highway 17, the road to Manila. On February 3 the 511th Parachute Infantry made an airdrop on Tagaytay Ridge, and soon the rest of the division coming along Highway 17 joined up on the ridge. Now the Eleventh Airborne was only 30 miles from Manila, but not coming fast enough for MacArthur, who had wanted to celebrate his sixty-fifth birthday in Manila.

All this while MacArthur was dashing from one sector of the front to another, keeping the pressure on Krueger to move faster, faster, faster. Krueger was extremely wary of all this because, unlike MacArthur, he correctly estimated the Japanese strength at more than 250,000 men, and, unlike MacArthur, he estimated also that Yamashita would try to defend Manila.

But there was a solid reason for MacArthur's haste. He had discovered that the beaches of Lingayen were not adequate to handle the huge buildup that would be necessary for the conquest of Luzon. The Clark Field complex would have to take care of an enormous load of air traffic. And, as soon as Manila was free of Japanese, the port of Manila would become the central staging area for supply. Meanwhile everything was in the works and had to be taken care of as it came, some way or other.

In the middle of January MacArthur's command and the Central Pacific command were involved in a serious quarrel over the naval units that MacArthur had been lent by the Pacific Fleet, which was now planning the Iwo Jima attack and needed to count on them. But MacArthur refused to send them back to Ulithi by January 19 for maintenance as promised. Since he had planned the two other flanking amphibious assaults after the first one, without consulting Nimitz, MacArthur insisted on retaining six battleships and 26 destroyers that belonged to the Pacific Fleet. He finally let two of the battleships go but the rest he did not release in time for the Iwo Jima assault, and later Pacific Fleet planners blamed MacArthur for heavy casualties at Iwo Jima because the navy did not have as much firepower as it should have had for the beach bombardment. It was probably a good thing for MacArthur that he would not need more cooperation in this regard from the Pacific Fleet because Nimitz was no longer inclined to trust his promises. It was a measure of MacArthur's obsession with the occupation of Manila that he would engage in such a quarrel, which could not help but damage his reputation for probity.

So the race for Manila began on February 1, sparked by MacArthur, between three divisions, the Thirty-seventh Infantry, the First Cavalry, and the Eleventh Airborne Division. Thirty-seventh Infantry Division had driven southward from Lingayen Gulf to Malolos where it was going to take the shoreline road, Highway 3, to Manila, 18 miles away.

The First Cavalry was north of Cabanatuan on Highway 5, some 70 miles north of Manila.

The Eleventh Airborne was 45 miles southwest of Manila.

General MacArthur visited the First Cavalry on January 30 and gave a little talk. He told them to go to Manila, to go around the Japanese; someone would take care of them later. He said to go to Manila, free the internees at Santo Tomas, and capture Malancanan Palace and the legislative building, which would symbolize a taking back the government. But in any event, said General MacArthur, hurry and get to Manila. The same idea was inculcated into the other two divisions. Manila, which had been founded by the Spanish in 1571, covered about 15 square miles and had a population of about 800,000 people. It extended from Grace Park south along the bay for 10 miles, to Paranaque. The port area covered the bay front for a mile on either side of the Pasig River. The main business district lay north of the river. Malancanan Palace, Old Bilibid Prison, and Santo Tomas University were in north Manila. South of the Pasig was the old walled city and its stone citadel, Fort Santiago. The old walled city was called Intramuros, and it was a wonder of its day, with walls 40 feet thick at the bottom and reaching the height of 25 feet, constructed of huge stone blocks, with the buildings inside the wall also constructed of formidable stone walls. Near the bay were many government buildings, and the commercial and residential areas of the new Manila. Fort McKinley and Neilson Field were just below the Pasig on the eastern edge of the city, and Nichols Field was three miles down the bay.

Major General V. D. Mudge, commander of the First Cavalry, listened to MacArthur's plea and then created two "flying columns" and sent them chasing down the road with orders to get to Manila and not stop for anything. They were to move out far ahead of the division.

Off they went. On February 1 the columns forded a river, swept through Cabanatuan, and sped south on Highway 5, leaving pockets of Japanese behind them. At Gapan the Japanese had set demolition charges under the bridge across the Penaradana River, but the flying columns hit them before they could blow the bridge, and then they were across and moving again. Thirty-seven miles south of Cabanatuan, the two flying columns separated to take different back roads to Manila. So far they had not faced any serious oposition. They found some bridges blown or destroyed by American air bombing, but they quickly found fords and moved on.

Near Novaliches, northeast of Manila, the men of one column arrived just as the Japanese were lighting the fuses of the demolition charges under a bridge. The Japanese fled. The cavalrymen grabbed the fuses and extinguished them, and the column dashed across the bridge on Route 52.

At Talipapali a Japanese road convoy approached the road to turn onto it. Troopers in the lead vehicles gestured to them to stop and the Japanese stopped. The column swooped by, shooting up the Japanese convoy and destroying some vehicles, but not even slowing down.

This column arrived at Grace Park, in the north of Manila, and crossed the city limits that evening of February 3. They were the first American troops to reenter the capital. They sped down Rizal Avenue, encountering a few astonished Japanese, and headed for Santo Tomas University. There they had a fight at the gates before they routed the guards and forced their way into the grounds. They liberated 3,700 civilian internees who had been held there since 1942. They moved on against increasing fire as the Japanese discovered that the enemy was on them. The seized Malancanan Palace on the north bank of the Pasig River and settled down. By February 5 the rest of the First Cavalry Division had arrived.

They had done as their general asked. They had gone to Manila and liberated the internees and captured the palace.

The Thirty-seventh Division had been in the race, but it had bogged down on the Manila shoreline by broken bridges and tidal streams. They also encountered strong fire from small groups of defenders. But they moved into Manila on February 4 and then went to Old Bilibid Prison, where they released about 500 civilian internees and 800 prisoners of war. The Japanese guards fled as the Americans came up.

The Eleventh Airborne traveled north on Highway 17 at high speed, bound for Manila. But four miles south of the city limits they were stopped at the Paranaque River by intense artillery mortar and machine gun fire. So they lost the race, but not for lack of effort. They had come up against the Genko Line, the defenses south of Nichols Field.

As the three American divisions had approached Manila it became apparent that the Japanese had strong forces in the city, although quite where no one was sure. General MacArthur had been right in one sense: General Yamashita had intended to abandon Manila without a fight, but the naval commander Admiral Iwabuchi had ignored Yamashita's orders to send the supplies and follow along into the mountains. He said he was going to defend Manila. He had 20,000 troops with which to defend the city.

So General Krueger was right. Finally there would be a fight for Manila. And it was just about to begin when the troops of the First Cavalry rushed in to free the internees and POWs, so fast that the Japanese were caught by surprise.

CHAPTER TWENTY-TWO

The Fight for Manila

The last reinforcements for the Japanese navy air force kamikaze corps were flown in from Formosa on December 23. And the last day of operations for the kamikazes of the First Air Fleet in the Philippines came on that January 5 attack from Mabalacat on the ships in Lingayen Gulf. After that the instructions were for most of the people involved with the First Air Fleet to become ground troops and serve under Admiral Iwabuchi in the defense of Manila.

Admiral Iwabuchi, who commanded the naval defense forces, was determined to defend Manila to the death. He thought the American attack would come from the south, and therefore only about 3,000 troops were put on the northern defense line around Grace Park. The others were dug in in the fortress of Intramuros, at Fort McKinley, and along the Genko Line in the south, The admiral brought in ship guns from damaged and sunken ships in Manila Harbor and placed them in the reinforced concrete buildings of his defense area. He also scavenged the ships for all other weapons, machine guns, mortars, and grenades. He got other weapons from the army stores. The naval stores yielded rockets, a new weapon in the Pacific, including some big 400-mm ones.

Most of his troops were not trained in infantry tactics, but they had enormous vitality, the will to fight to the death, weapons, and strongly fortified buildings, particularly in the old city of Manila. It was their announced purpose to make every shot count, to make the taking of Manila as expensive for the Americans as possible, and thus to delay the conquest of the Philippines and the day when the blow would fall within the inner Japanese empire.

Not knowing all this, the troops of the Thirty-seventh Infantry Division and the First Cavalry Division came down from the north to Manila and moved to west and east sides of the city to begin clearing out the Japanese. Iwabuchi's detachment destroyed all the military supplies and facilities in the north port area and in San Nicolas and Binondo, and then withdrew across the Pasig River, blowing up the bridges as they went. The flames, fanned by the wind, spread into the slum district of Tondo and burned, with fires so clearly visible that General Eichelberger could see them eight miles away. On the night of February 5 the troops of the Thirty-seventh Division turned firefighter and spent two days putting out the fires in the city of Manila.

The Thirty-seventh Division then cleaned out the Japanese corners of resistance on the bay side of the Pasig River and secured the part of the water supply system for the city there. By February 10 the Thirty-seventh had secured the western half of north Manila and the First Cavalry had secured the eastern half. About 1,500 Japanese and 50 Americans had been killed in this action.

South of Manila the heavy fighting was between the Eleventh Airborne troops around Nichols Field and General Tsukada's troops, who had joined the Iwabuchi defenders.

As usual the MacArthur propaganda machine was going full blast. On February 6 his headquarters announced, "Our forces are rapidly clearing the enemy from Manila. Our converging columns entered the city and surrounded the Jap defenders. Their complete destruction is imminent."

That communique sounded reminiscent of the communiques issuing from Imperial General Headquarters in Tokyo three and a half years earlier when General Homma spent almost five months conquering the Americans and every day Tokyo was reporting "imminent" victory. All of which proves that the Japanese had no corner on impetuous and misleading propaganda.

Within hours, the expected congratulatory messages came in from President Roosevelt, Secretary of State Henry L. Stimson, Prime Minister Curtin of Australia, Generalissimo Chiang Kai-shek, Winston Churchill. The result was very pleasing to MacArthur. He met his generals in Manila and visited Bilibid to talk to the freed prisoners there. He visited Santo Tomas to see the civilian internees who had just been liberated., He received dramatic thanks and ovations from all. He went to inspect Malancanan Palace and visited the lines on the Pasig River. He retrieved his Cadillac car that he had left on Corregidor and that had since been the staff car of the Japanese commander in Manila.

He drove through Manila and was lionized by the Filipinos; men, women, and children literally danced in the streets. On February 10 he announced a giant victory parade to be held, in which he would lead the troops through the streets of Manila.

It was all very satisfying.

But there was a catch. MacArthur had not consulted Admiral Iwabuchi and did not know that the Japanese had no intention of surrendering.

It was not all over. It was not almost all over. In fact, as became painfully obvious, it was just beginning.

Four days after the announcement of the triumphal parade, the plan was suddenly canceled.

Those four days had begun with MacArthur going down to watch the 148th Infantry board assault boats and cross the Pasig River near Malacanan Palace on February 7. The attack had cost 115 casualties, which did not seem too high; a foothold had been gained on the south bank and soon other units of the Thirty-seventh Division were across and in the buildings and streets of the Pandacan District. They were moving toward the Paco District and the Intramuros. And here the advance stopped.

Japanese strong points on Provisor Island and nearby

buildings began to erupt fire from machine guns and artillery, and the American infantry was pinned down. The generals asked to use air strikes, and MacArthur refused to let them. He said they could not even use artillery, but when told that then they could not advance, he relented on the artillery but not on the air strikes. He was not yet prepared to face the fact that the Japanese had double-crossed him and deprived him of the triumph that he expected. The rooting out of the Japanese was going to be a slow and bloody business.

The field artillery of the Thirty-seventh Division began to turn the buildings of the Provisor area into rubble. Building by building they fought for the blocks. Meanwhile the First Cavalry was driving toward the suburb of Pasay on Manila Bay.

In the south the Eleventh Airborne troops were making no progress on February 4. On February 10 the artillery came in to help them, and on the 11th they captured Nichols Field. Four days later the Eleventh Airborne linked up with the First Cavalry, which meant that Iwabuchi's forces were encircled within Manila.

Inside Manila the First Cavalry was reducing the works at Fort McKinley. On February 19 the job was finished. Admiral Iwabuchi had made his headquarters there, but he escaped to Intramuros. General Yokoyama, the army commander in the mountains of the east, said he would make a counterattack in the Novaliches area to enable the navy contingent to escape to the mountains. He did attack but Iwabuchi made no attempt to escape; instead he strengthened his defenses in Intramuros.

The Eleventh Airborne turned south and took the old Cavite Naval Station. Other troops took Neilson Field. The Thirty-seventh Infantry and the First Cavalry moved against Intramuros. The fighting moved to old Manila landmarks up Dewey Boulevard: the Army Navy Club, the Manila Hotel, the Philippine General Hospital. The Japanese were holed up in all of these. To the east the Thirty-seventh cleared the post office, the new police station, and city hall.

By February 22 the Japanese had been driven into the northeast corner of South Manila, Intramuros, and the commonwealth government buildings near the old walled city.

By this time the Americans had suffered very heavy casualties in the fighting and thousands of Japanese were dead—most of the 20,000 defenders. The city had been laid waste from Pasay to the Pasig River. In the hysteria of the final days of resistance the Japanese high command lost control of the troops who embarked on a frenzy reminiscent of the Nanking massacre. When the Americans neared Intramuros they came upon piles of Filipino bodies—men, women, and children. Some of the women had obviously been raped before being killed. Many of the thousands of bodies had their hands tied behind their backs. It was claimed that the Japanese killed 100,000 Filipino civilians in those last days, although there is evidence that a great number of them were killed by fire between Japanese and Americans and perhaps even by American shelling.

MacArthur learned at about this time of the Palawan massacre. Guards at a prison camp on Palawan Island thought that a convoy bound for Mindoro was coming to their island, and they panicked and herded American prisoners of war into underground shelters, set them alight with gasoline, and then machine gunned them. They killed 140 men, but nine somehow survived to tell the tale. MacArthur also learned of a large internment camp the Japanese kept at Los Banos, 30 miles southwest of Manila, on Lagune de Bay. The Eleventh Airborne was told; they attacked Los Banos, killed the Japanese garrison, and resuced 2,300 internees who might otherwise have been massacred in those days of frenetic resistance.

By mid-February the Americans were calling on the Japanese trapped in the Intramuros to surrender, but they got no response. The Japanese would not surrender and would not release the Filipinos they held hostage inside their defense perimeter. Major General O. W. Griswold, the corps commander, asked General Krueger for bombing of Intramuros. MacArthur came down hard and flatly refused to allow the bombing of the city, but he did agree to a massive artillery bombardment, which was not much different. From February 17 to 23 the Americans used every available piece of artillery, and so heavy was the shelling that it finally broke those thick walls on the northeast corner. Troops began to move into the Intramuros, fighting all the way. Other troops began to take the government buildings near the Intramuros. It was March 3 before General Griswold reported that the fighting in Manila had finally come to an end. The Thirty-seventh Division counted nearly 17,000 dead Japanese and claimed to have killed most of them with casualties of about 1,200 for the Thirty-seventh and the Eleventh Airborne. About six Filipinos died for every American or Japanese soldier. And Manila, which MacArthur said the Japanese would not defend, lay a wreck, with the downtown in shambles and the transportation and public health facilities destroyed or paralyzed.

MacArthur had already toured war-torn Manila in mid-February. But for months he and the Philippine government would have to cope with the problems of bringing the city back to life.

On February 27 a ceremony was held at Malancanan Palace to mark the reestablishment of the Philippine Commonwealth government in Manila. Osmena made a speech, and MacArthur made a very emotional speech. The whole of the Manila experience had been shattering to him, especially his return to his former home, a penthouse in the Manila Hotel where the ensconced Japanese had resisted to the last, and so the hotel was almost completely wrecked; he found his library gone and his memorabilia destroyed. His beloved Manila where he had spent so much of his life since childhood was in ruins.

On March 5 General MacArthur moved his headquarters into Manila.

Now came the final act in the return to Manila: the siege of Corregidor, which meant so much to the Americans who had fought and bled there in 1942. Since January 22 the fortress had been under almost constant bombardment. How to seize the fortress from the Japanese?

The Allied leaders knew that the Japanese had lost about half their force in assaulting Corregidor from the sea in 1942, and MacArthur did not want to repeat the performance. He decided on a combined air-sea assault, using the 503rd Parachute Regiment and a battalion of the Twenty-fourth Division coming from the sea. The airdrop was very tenuous; the target was small and miscalculation would send them onto the rocks below.

Once again MacArthur's intelligence officers did not serve him well. They estimated that there were only 900 Japanese on the Rock, and there were actually 5,000 to 6,000 enemy troops.

The assault came on February 16.

Colonel George M. Jones, the commander of the 503rd Parachute Infantry Regiment, had been named commander of the "Rock Force," which would assault Corregidor. The main assault would be made by three battalions of paratroops and one battalion of the Thirty-fourth Regular Infantry, which would come in by sea.

Corregidor was going to be difficult; everyone knew that. The island is long and narrow, three and a half miles long and one and a half miles across at the widest point. The eastern end is sandy and wooded, 150 feet above Manila Bay. At the center of the island is Malinta Hill, which rises to 350 feet. West of Malinta Hill the ground falls away to an area known as Bottomside, which is only a hundred feet above the water. Along the north and south sides are sandy beaches, admirable for assault. West of Bottomside lies a rise called Middleside that leads west to the steep slope whose top is known as Topside.

On February 6 Colonel Jones flew over Corregidor in a bomber. He did not see any evidence of Japanese defenders, which encouraged him to believe that the GHQ estimate of 800 to 900 soldiers only must be correct. On that basis

Colonel Jones made his plan. At 8:30 on D-Day a third of his paratroopers would bail out over Topside. They would aim at the golf course and the parade grounds. Lieutenant Colonel John Erickson's Third Battalion would be entrusted to clear away the Japanese on Topside and to cover the amphibious troops' assault on Black Beach at Bottomside. Then in the afternoon the Second Battalion would jump. And the following day the First Battalion would come in.

What a place to jump!

Each zone was only about 400 feet wide and 1,000 feet long. The ground was littered with boulders, bomb craters, scrap-iron debris, and old tin roofing. The golf course was full of splintered trees, and a half-demolished barracks and other buildings stood among the obstacles. If the wind was blowing, and it most certainly would be, men ran the risk of being blown out past the drop zone and down into the cliffs or into Manila Bay. But there was no other way. They had to accept the probably high casualties of the air drop. They would use a strange drop technique. Each troop carrier aircraft would make several passes, and six men would drop from each plane each time. This was only possible because the Americans had air and naval superiority now, but it would minimize the losses.

On the day before the assault a flotilla of American cruisers, destroyers, and landing craft carried the landing troops to Bataan at Mariveles, three miles west of Corregidor. They then began bombarding the fortress island, which had already been hit by 3,000 tons of bombs in the recent days.

That night the Japanese island commander, Captain Akira Itagaki, sent 30 suicide boats to attack the American ships. Eighteen boats got lost but 12 attacked and sank three gunboats patroling the entrance to Mariveles Harbor. They also damaged one landing craft.

On the morning of D-Day Admiral Berkey's cruiser began a new bombardment of Corregidor, and the bombers came again to drop fragmentation bombs to keep the Japanese defenders inside the tunnels of the Rock. Then the planes, which had taken off from Mindoro, began to come in with the paratroops.

At 8:33 they began to drop.

Lieutenant Colonel Erickson jumped from 500 feet, and the 24-mile-per-hour wind carried him far from his objective, to Wheeler Battery, the site of an American shore gun position of the old days when American guns had guarded Manila Bay. He dropped his parachute and walked back to the battalion assembly point.

Some men fell into the wrecked buildings. Some fell into bomb craters. Some caught their parachutes in trees and dangled. One stick of eight men landed in front of a cave filled with Japanese and were cut down before they could get out of their parachute harnesses. One trooper whose parachute failed splattered into the empty concrete swimming pool of the golf club. Some troopers were impaled on splintered trees and steel poles.

The paratroops had 280 jump casualties, including one of the two doctors and both the Catholic and the Protestant chaplains. Actually the wounded or injured were many more, but if a man had only a sprained ankle or other injury—if he could still function and still fight—then almost all of these walking wounded kept on going. The casualty list for the jump will never really be known because morale was high and the men wanted to get a very difficult job done.

Circling above in a command plane and watching the problems of the first jump, Colonel Jones ordered the rest of the men dropped at 400 feet so they would not blow away and the percentage of safe drops would be improved. Colonel Jones was the first to bail out at the lower altitude, which barely allowed time for the parachute to open before the man hit the ground. Colonel Jones landed in a shell-splintered tree, and a piece of the tree penetrated his inner thigh. He managed to break off the piece of wood and pull it out, got out of his tree and his parachute, and limped toward his command post. He did not regard himself as a casualty, although a medical officer would have done so.

Several troopers landed near Wheeler Point, not far from the old lighthouse. There in a cave on Topside, a most exposed position, was the Japanese command post, headed by Captain Akira Itagaki. The paratroops saw movement and realized it was enemy. Not knowing that this was the nerve center of the whole defense, they hurled grenades into the cave. They heard shouts and screams, and then silence.

The Americans found dead enemy officers inside the cave, and one of them was identified as Captain Itagaki. The others were key members of his staff. So by sheer luck, in the opening hours of the battle the American paratroopers had wiped out the command structure of the defense. There-after it was not a coordinated defense but a series of violent actions of Japanese groups who had nothing left but death with honor and who were hoping to make the price as high as possible.

The men kept coming down and it became apparent on the ground that the casualty figures from the air drop did not really tell the story. Nearly all the 1,000 men who dropped had some sort of injury. But 750 of them were able to keep fighting. They thought now that they about matched the number of Japanese, but that it would still be tough going because the enemy had the advantage of the Corregidor defensive system. It was not until after the battle that they learned what they really faced: There were actually about 6,000 enemy troops on the island. Had Cap-tain Itagaki not perished in the early action on Topside, the price the Americans would have had to pay for Corregidor might have been much, much higher.

The battalion of the Thirty-fourth Infantry was brought in to Black Beach by 25 landing ships medium (LSM) and they landed there at Bottomside, with orders to charge up the 400-foot-high Malinta Hill and seize control, thus cutting the Japanese forces in two. The Japanese who had been in the tunnel and caves went to their guns and opened fire on the landing craft, causing many casualties. On Black Beach the troops ran into mines. Mortar fire and mines kept them pinned down. In half an hour they had lost half their vehicles to mines and antitank fire from the cliffs.

But soon Topside and Malinta Hill were both in American hands. At the end of the first day about 2,500 Americans were on the beach and on top of Corregidor's tunnels. And in the tunnels and caves were nearly 6,000 Japanese who were ready to die, but not alone if they could help it.

Soon small groups of Japanese began to move about Topside and the 2,000 paratroopers and paratroop artillerymen were in action. As night fell and quiet came, the Japanese soldiers began emerging from their tunnels and caves. They attacked an aid station and other spots. Shortly after midnight they mortared Malinta Hill. Then the Japanese marines attacked Malinta Hill but the Americans held, and with the arrival of dawn the Japanese disappeared with their wounded, down into the tunnels again.

That first night the Japanese also launched a banzai charge on Black Beach but the infantrymen held them off and then killed all of them.

Dawn opened with an American tank lumbering up to Malinta tunnel and firing inside. Thirty-five Japanese came running out and into the fire of the American paratroops.

In the last few passes on the day before the C-47s had been hit by a lot of shellfire, so on this second day Colonel Jones canceled the second paradrop. The men's equipment was dropped but they came in by boat. It was a wise decision—of the 44 planes making the flight 16 were hit by gunfire. If the paratroopers had dropped from those planes the Japanese gunners would have filled the air with heavy antiaircraft fire and the casualties would have been very heavy.

It was bad enough because the Japanese in cliffside caves attacked as the paratroops came into Black Beach by boat, but the destroyer *Claxton* edged up and began firing into the caves and the Japanese gunners quit.

The fighting on Topside was fierce. The Japanese at Wheeler Battery on the edge of the cliff lived in underground magazines, and an attempt to capture one that that day cost F Company three of its six officers. The Americans used flamethrowers and white phosphorous grenades to rout the Japanese from the caves.

The second night came, and the Japanese again emerged from the mountain to make banzai attacks. They hit Malinta Hill and very nearly took it. By dawn only three Americans of K Company were still on their feet, but that morning they counted 150 Japanese corpses around their position.

That day a new tactic emerged. The Americans would work in patrols by daylight, digging out the Japanese, using all the devices at their command. At dusk they would pull back into a perimeter and guard it during the night. They had to expect one surprise attack after another.

After this second night Colonel Jones realized that the MacArthur intelligence report on the number of Japanese on the Rock had been seriously in error. In two days they had already killed the 800 Japanese estimated and there were hundreds more down in the bowels of the Rock, he knew. By D-Day plus two the fortress was beginning to stink. Several ammunition dumps inside had been blown up, and the corpses were rotting. Also 800 known dead were strewn about the island, bloating and growing black. Bulldozers were brought in to bury the dead. Some were pushed into Manila Bay. The flies, feeding on the dead, became such a nuisance that some men could not eat. So each day a plane came over loaded with DDT and sprayed the island to keep the flies down.

One device the soldiers invented in this fight was a hanging bomb, made from a five-gallon can filled with napalm, to which eight white phosphorous grenades were fixed. Around this was placed a fuse and several blocks of dynamite. The fuse time was fixed for 15 minutes. It was put down into a magazine that held 80,000 pounds of explosive, and when it went off so did the magazine with an enormous roar and a huge black cloud. A number of Japanese so met their ancestors.

Another night came, and in the early hours of D-Day plus three the Japanese erupted again. At one point, a number of Americans were bivouacked on top of an underground Japanese amunition dump. That night the Japanese blew it up, killing 20 Japanese, but also an equal number of Americans on top of them. Some others came out and killed themselves with grenades.

That night the Imperial Marines staged a really coordinated banzai attack at Wheeler Point. Eighty-five of them captured a building atop the Rock and were blasted out by pack howitzers the next day. All 85 were killed by artillery fire.

By February 21 the Japanese were growing desperate. They were out of water and their force was split in two. That day the Japanese planned a limited explosion to put the Americans off guard for a new attack, but the explosion got out of hand and several hundred Japanese were killed. It might have been worse. From captured documents, Colonel Jones estimated that the Japanese had enough explosives down there to blow up the whole Rock. It was small arms ammunition, mortar rounds, artillery shells, grenades, and hundreds of tons of dynamite even after the 80,000-pound explosion.

The fight went on and on and on. There was no easy way. On February 23, D-Day plus seven, Colonel Jones got a report that the Japanese had lost 2,500 men to date. The American casualties were 118 killed and 314 wounded.

But those casualties would soon rise. On the morning of February 26 the Japanese blew up a magazine at Monkey Point when many Americans were on top of the position. It was a catastrophe, with 196 paratroops killed or wounded, and about 200 Japanese.

The Japanese fought fiercely but without organization, launching banzai charges and wasting men. In three days they lost 1,500 men. But they still controlled the caves and tunnels of Corregidor. Every day was almost like that night of February 21 when the Japanese suddenly erupted in the tunnel below Malinta Hill, committing mass suicide, setting off ammunition and explosives. The explosions blew rocks and debris in all directions and produced many landslides, some of which trapped and killed American troops on the surface. Almost every night the performance was repeated and more Japanese died until that February 26 explosion when the surviving Japanese on Monkey Point blew up an underground arsenal, killing another 200 of their own people but also about 50 Americans who were on top of the hill.

Finally on March 1 Colonel Jones, the commander of the 503rd Parachute Infantry, reported that organized resistance on the island had ended. The Americans had taken 20 prisoners, but all the rest of the 6,000-man garrison was dead.

Next came the mopping up of Japanese survivors all around Manila Bay. One of the hot spots was Ternate on the southern shore of the bay, where the Eleventh Airborne encountered some 350 Japanese and had a fierce firefight before vanquishing and killing them.

On April 13 the Thirty-eighth Division encountered a small enemy garrison on the island of Caballo and routed them by pouring thousands of gallons of fuel oil into the tunnel ventilators and then setting fire to them. not a pretty sort of warfare, but the Japanese refused to give up, and for an American to enter the tunnels was to court death. The Thirty-eighth Division men did the same thing at the island of El Fraile southwest of Corregidor. The last stronghold on the island of Carabao was bombarded for two days from the sea, and then a detachment of the Thirty-eighth Division landed—and captured the sole living inhabitant, a shell-shocked pig. The Japanese garrison had gone weeks before—another failure for MacArthur's very sloppy intelligence system under Major General Charles A. Willoughby, who seemed to hold his job only because he was one of the loyal handful of men around MacArthur from the beginning days in Manila.

By March 16 the Manila Harbor had been cleaned up so that it could be used by Allied ships, if on a limited basis. They found 300 ships sunk in the harbor, dating back to the first Japanese bombing and increased manyfold by subsequent American attacks on the bay. The port facilities were a total disaster. It would be months before Manila could be restored by the efforts of American engineers.

MacArthur spent a considerable amount of time making symbolic gestures. On March 2 after the fighting ended on Corregidor, he and members of his staff boarded four PT boats (which was the same number that went out with MacArthur in the spring of 1942), and journeyed to Corregidor. MacArthur inspected the scenes of fighting and his old tunnel office, which had been ruined in the Japanese destruction, and supervised a flag-raising ceremony. MacArthur made one of his emotional speeches to Colonel Jones and his men:

> Colonel Jones, the capture of Corregidor is one of the most brilliant operations in military history. Outnumbered two to one [which Willoughby had not known] your command by its unfaltering courage, its invincible determination, and its professional skill, overcame all obstacles and annihilated the enemy. I have cited to the order of the day all units involved and I take great pride in awarding you as their commander the Distinguished Service Cross as a symbol of the fortitude, devotion, and the bravery with which you have fought. I see the old flagpole still stands. Have your troops hoist the colors to its peak and let no enemy ever haul them down again.

And so the fight for Corregidor ended. The 503rd Parachute Infantry Regiment had won the day with a lot of help from the Thirty-fourth Infantry and the army air corps, the navy, and the marines. They had suffered 223 men killed and 1,107 wounded, a casualty rate of one-third of the force.

So Manila and all the important landmarks that symbolized the beginning of the war were now taken, but General Yamashita was still fighting, with nearly 200,000 men in the northern Philippines, plus all the garrisons of all the islands that had been bypassed in the rush to Manila. The job of rebuilding Manila began, and at the same time the war went on. It would be a hard struggle, for General Yamashita was determined to make the Americans pay a very stiff price for victory. But it was time to get on with it.

CHAPTER TWENTY-THREE

MacArthur's Return

Early in March all the fighting had ended in and around Manila and the Filipino people could begin to pick up their lives and try to do something about their shattered city.

General MacArthur began to put his life together again, too, and he was not unmindful of the problems of the people. Although the fighting had not stopped, but rather increased in the mountains south of Baguio and east of Manila, General MacArthur assigned a large number of troops to help clear the debris out of the city and restore the essential services for life. Relief supplies came in from America and were quickly distributed. Medical team cared for public health and averted epidemics. Makeshift classrooms were found and teachers began to teach school again. The army engineers repaired the city water system. Engineers began to work on the port facilities. By early April a supply depot at Manila was functioning and handling hundreds of thousands of tons of supplies.

Because the venereal disease rate among the American troops began to go up, the doctors recommended that General MacArthur put Manila off limits to the American troops, but he refused to do so, saying that the money the soldiers spent was bringing new economic life to the city.

By March 13, less than two weeks after the fighting ended, the lights began to go on again all over Manila. On March 15 General MacArthur took another of his symbolic trips. He and staff members went by jeep to Caloocan and took the train that ran back to Manila. The train was decked with flags and passed through cheering crowds. General MacArthur made a short speech at the Manila railway station, praising the Filipino and American workers who had gotten the line between Manila and Lingayen Gulf into operation so quickly. Soon there were more semblances of normal life, including concerts by municipal bands.

For General MacArthur there was a good deal of pain involved in the homecoming. His Cadillac limousine was found on the grounds of Santo Tomas University, where the Japanese commandant had used it and made the internees build a special garage for it. The general's library had been scattered. Some of it may have been sent to Tokyo. Engineers found his set of the Cambridge Modern History series in the debris of the Manila Hotel. The MacArthur silver service was found in an office building near Malancanan.

General MacArthur moved his advance headquarters to the Wilson Building in North Manila. He found a house—rather he let General Kenney find the house—Casa Blanca, which belonged to the Bachrach family—and then MacArthur took it away from Kenney. It was a mansion in the exclusive Santa Mesa district, less than a mile from the Malancanan Palace and near the north bank of the Pasig River. Kenney came out all right in the matter; he found an even better house and would not tell MacArthur where it was located.

MacArthur's wife, Jean, and his son left Brisbane by ship on February 21 and arrived in Manila on March 6. She then began a busy life of social work in a city that needed it badly.

General Krueger, who was soon promoted to four-star general, wanted to get right to work destroying General Yamashita's Fourteenth Area Army, but MacArthur had other plans. He saw that if Yamashita was penned into the mountains of northern Luzon there was not a great deal of damage he could do, particularly since he had no aircraft left. Thus MacArthur could devote some of the energy of the command to clearing pockets and centers of resistance in the Southern Philippines.

The problem for General Krueger was that by reducing his Sixth Army from its 11 divisions and four regimental combat teams, MacArthur made it impossible for Krueger to bring decisive force to bear on the Shimbu and Shobu groups, which had been set up independent of Krueger's divisions to General Eichelberger's Eighth Army, which was going to take the central and southern Philippines. It began with an assault on Palawan on February 28.

General MacArthur's reason for this approach was to clear southern Luzon to secure the shoreline and make it possible for troop ships to use the San Bernardino Strait route from Leyte to Luzon. This was 500 miles shorter than the route through the Sulu and South China seas. Another reason was to set up a new supply base at Batangas Bay to relieve the pressure on the Manila base.

And still another reason, and one that would dog the Americans in the future and place them—in Asian eyes—in the forefront of the "Imperialists" was MacArthur's intention to reestablish Dutch rule of the Dutch East Indies and to help the British and French take over their old imperial possessions. This was all low-key and most Americans were not even aware of it, but in the last months of the war, the political elements of the future struggles of Asians for independence began to emerge, and General MacArthur was either oblivious or unsympathetic to them.

Thus as the Japanese were to be driven out of all the territories in southeast Asia that they had invested, General MacArthur, without the knowledge of the top American leadership, was quietly manipulating the future of the Philippines and of Southeast Asia in the manner he believed it should go.

NOTES

1 The Road to Australia

The material for the first chapter of this book came from the MacArthur Memorial Archives in Norfolk, Virginia, which is also the source of the original material for volume 4 of this series, *The Jungles of New Guinea*. Some of the material came from reports of air activity in the Philippine islands in the early days of the war, saved by General Whitney.

2 New Guinea Operations

General MacArthur was obviously the victim of misinformation. When he went to Australia he believed that he was being chosen to lead the American war effort in the Pacific. But this did not turn out to be true, and instead of becoming the key figure in the defense plans, he was reduced to a secondary role as commander of what was really a backwater in the Southwest Pacific area. This was largely because Admiral King preempted the role of leadership, seeing the great danger in the Japanese buildup of the Solomon Islands as a major threat to Allied communications and insisting on stopping it with the invasion of Guadalcanal, which General MacArthur opposed. So in August 1942 the scene switched from the southwest to the South Pacific and MacArthur lost his leadership role, which he would not regain until the summer of 1944 when President Roosevelt would finally opt, for political and historical reasons, to return to the Philippines rather than choose to go to Formosa or the China coast, the route wanted by the navy. The problems of the Southwest Pacific campaign in New Guinea are more specifically described in volume 4 of this series, *The Jungles of New Guinea*. In this volume they simply serve as background material to offset the burden of the book, which is MacArthur's road back to the Philippines.

3 The New War

The movement up the coast of New Guinea to Hollandia and Biak was contested by the Japanese, but they were really looking for that "great decisive battle," and the opportunity never presented itself in the MacArthur sphere, largely because the Japanese saw that the basic problem was the existence and growing power of the American Pacific Fleet, and they exerted their major efforts to bring that fleet to battle. But when they succeeded in the summer of 1944, they had nearly exhausted their resources in the naval field. Their carrier fleet was diminished and, more important, their pilot training program had lagged far beyond the demands of the South Pacific and so they did not have the trained pilots to win the battle of the Philippine Sea, although they were lucky and skillful enough to achieve the first strike. But that first strike spelled disaster to Admiral Ozawa. The Americans called it the Marianas Turkey Shoot, referring to an American backwoods sport that is like shooting fish in a barrel. The Japanese pilots were too inept, and the American planes were too many.

4 Attack to the North

The basic source for this chapter is the MacArthur collection in the Norfolk archives.

5 Heading for the Philippines

Again the MacArthur archives were the primary source, with the James book in support. The references to Admiral Halsey come from my studies for *The Glory of the Solomons*, published by Stein and Day in 1978. It is mistakenly believed that MacArthur met with President Roosevelt and Admiral Nimitz in Hawaii and immediately charmed Roosevelt into changing the master plan for the Pacific war to direct it to the Philippines. Actually nothing was decided at that meeting, although Roosevelt was impressed by MacArthur's arguments.

6 Divided Commands

The story of the Eichelberger-Krueger controversy comes from the MacArthur archives and from James. Eichelberger was obviously very jealous of Krueger's successes and position.

7 Changes

In Admiral Halsey's roving attacks on the Philippines in September, 1944 he drew the conclusion that Japanese air power was virtually wiped out. This conclusion was based on a faulty perception. The Japanese navy air force was responsible for air defense of the Philippines, and it was in bad shape. But the Japanese army air force had more than 2,500 aircraft in the Philippines, which they were saving for army operations. Thus the Americans would be surprised after the invasion of Leyte by the strength of the Japanese air attacks against the beachhead and the troop installations. Halsey's conclusions are from studies of mine for various books, especially *The Battle of Leyte Gulf*. Also, the decision to invade the Palaus had been bypassed by events. The decision was made on the basis that the Japanese fleet had moved from Truk to Palau, but by the time the Americans invaded, it had moved again, this time to be centered at Lingga Roads, near Singapore. MacArthur's promise to conquer the Philippines in six weeks was based on another faulty premise about the strength of the Japanese army, which MacArthur's intelligence chief consistently underrated.

The decision by Admiral Halsey to go after the Japanese fleet if given a chance was made long before the battle of Surigao Strait. The only real question, which no one answered, was which was the really important aspect of the Japanese fleet, the carrier force or the battleship force. There was no way that Halsey could have known that the carrier force, which he chose, had been completely crippled by the diversion of aircraft to the Philippines and Formosa.

8 October Uncertainties

The Sho plan, which I studied for *The Battle of Leyte Gulf*, was the Japanese navy's last gasp and was thoroughly criticized by the Japanese army as destroying the "fleet in being" in a useless cause that could not possibly succeed. In this case the army turned out to be right. After the Philippines battles, the American navy no longer worried about the Japanese fleet elements. The big problem became the kamikazes, and that was one problem that the American navy never solved. The discussions of Japanese air power in this chapter come largely from materials gathered for *The Kamikazes*, which was published by Arbor House in 1984. The story of Admiral Halsey's attack on Taiwan is from *The Battle of Leyte Gulf*, and from materials gathered for *McCampbell's Heroes*, published by Van Nostrand Reinhold in 1981. The descriptions of the operations of the T Attack Force come from Admiral Fukudome's essay in *The Japanese Navy in World War II*. The discussion of the reactions in Tokyo to the battle of Taiwan comes from the *Boei* series, the *Japan Times* for October 1944, and the Fukudome essay.

9 On the Way to Leyte

The material about the defense of the Philippines by the Japanese is from the *Boei* series volume on the Japanese army defenses and from James. The material about the Sho plan operations and the various forces involved is from materials collected for *The Battle of Leyte Gulf*. The quotations from General MacArthur come from materials in the archives. Much of the material about the landings is from Morison's volume on Leyte and from an interview with Admiral Kinkaid some years ago in Washington.

10 Landing at Leyte

The story of the Leyte landings is from Morison for the most part. Part of the material about American army operations comes from the Breuer book. The story of MacArthur's hours ashore on Leyte is from James. The story of Admiral Ohnishi in the Philippines is from his records, materials gathered for *The Kamikazes*, and *The Divine Wind* by Rikihei Inoguchi and Tadashi Nakajima.

11 The Japanese Move

The material about the suicide squads is from materials collected for *The Kamikazes*. The story of Marshal Terauchi's change in plans is from the *Boei* Japanese army volume. Part of the story of the Kurita force is from the diary of Admiral Matome Ugaki. The story of the *Dace* and *Darter* is from Morison. The story of Admiral Ozawa is from *The Battle of Leyte Gulf*. The story of MacArthur at Tacloban is from James. The story of Admiral Fukudome's operations is from *The Kamikazes*. The story of the American defense is largely from *McCampbell's Heroes*.

12 The Battle of the Sibuyan Sea

The story of the battle of the Sibuyan Sea comes from Morison and *The Battle of Leyte Gulf*. The Japanese side is told by Admiral Ugaki in his diary, and in the *Boei* series.

13 The Decoy

The story of Admiral Ozawa's operations is from *The Battle of Leyte Gulf*.

14 The Battle of Surigao Strait

The story of Surigao Strait is from Barbey's book, the interview with Admiral Kinkaid, and *The Battle of Leyte Gulf*. Part of the story of Surigao Strait comes from *The Japanese Navy in World War II*. The story of the destroyers' part in the battle is from Morison.

15 Shima Arrives

The story of the misadventures of the Shima force is from Morison and *The Battle of Leyte Gulf*.

16 The Battle of Samar

The story of the battle of Samar comes from Morison, *The Men of the Gambier Bay* (my book about the escort carrier that was lost in the battle to the guns of the Japanese cruisers), and from the Ugaki diaries. For *The Battle of Leyte Gulf* I went into the record of the Pacific Fleet and Seventh Fleet forces in considerable detail to show the brave effort made by the destroyers and escorts, so brave that the Japanese thought they were fighting cruisers.

17 The Kamikazes

This chapter comes from *The Divine Wind* and *The Kamikazes*. In the original research for *The Kamikazes* I made extensive use of the biography of Admiral Ohnishi and I used some of that material here. The effect of the kamikaze attacks on the American forces is well indicated by Morison, and I have used his material here.

18 The Phantom Carriers

The story of Admiral Ozawa's desperate and fruitless journey is from the *Boei* series, research for *The Battle of Leyte*

Gulf, and Morison. The controversy about Halsey's decision to go after the carriers was at its height in the 1950s and 1960s and I discussed it with Admiral Carney, Halsey's chief of staff, with Admiral Kinkaid, and with many others. Naval people remain sharply divided, some thinking Halsey was rash and some thinking he did precisely the right thing. I go back to the words of Lord Nelson, who said once that any captain who laid his vessel (or force) alongside the enemy and fought could not be doing too much wrong. Fighting and the destruction of the enemy was the purpose of navy vessels. In the American successes in World War II the protective instinct came to the fore, and Admiral Spruance was the epitome of the thinking that saving the landing was everything and risking the fleet was dangerous. That was a proper view as long as the enemy was so far inferior that he could not attack from the rear. Spruance was lucky, but not aggressive. Perhaps the war would not have ended sooner if he had let Admiral Mitscher engage the Japanese carrier fleet in June 1944 as Mitscher wanted to do, but I happen to believe it might have. So one could say that in the matter of the battle of Cape Engano I am a supporter of Admiral Halsey's decision.

19 Leyte Operations

The material about General MacArthur in this chapter is from the James biography. The stories about Ohnishi and the Japanese are from materials I first used in *The Kamikazes*. The material about General Kenney's decisions is from *We Shall Return* by William M. Leary. Much of the material about the land operations is from the Breuer book, and some is from the MacArthur archives. Some of the material about General Hodge and the Twenty-fourth Corps is from discussions with General Hodge and his staff officers at a later time. The story about the Japanese attack on the airfields is from Breuer and James. The stories of the problems of the seagoing fighters are from Morison.

20 Mindoro

The Nimitz-MacArthur controversy is delineated in Morison. The Mindoro invasion was costly, as indicated by Morison, James, and others, but it was worthwhile because without a land base for the aircraft MacArthur would never have been able to get his Fifth Air Force into action, which it alternatively did not do in the Leyte campaign. But the navy had to put up with the new war that the Japanese had created in their decision to use their aircraft to destroy ships, particularly warships and most particularly carriers to slow down the American advance on Japan.

21 The Rush to Manila

The MacArthur planning of the invasion of Luzon is clearly told in James and Morison. The operation is described in both in detail, and in Breuer as well. I used the James tales of the drive of the various divisions. James was particularly effective in presenting MacArthur's almost frenetic activity to move the drive to Manila along faster. The story of the movement of the various divisions is from all these sources.

22 The Fight for Manila

The material about the Japanese naval air force comes from *The Kamikazes*. The story of the cancellation of the triumphal Manila parade is from James. Most of the other tales in the chapter come from Breuer and James.

23 MacArthur's Return

The material used in this chapter again comes from James, Morrison and Brewer.

BIBLIOGRAPHY

My primary source for this book were the records of General MacArthur and his command in the MacArthur Memorial Archives in Norfolk, Virginia, which I also used as a primary source for volume 4 of this series, *The Jungles of New Guinea*. As biographer Clayton James said, there is disappointingly little about MacArthur personally there. But that is true of his memoirs, too. What he did say seems much more important than what he did not say.

The fact is, however, that the controversial areas of MacArthur's career are only peripheral to this book. I dealt with one controversial area in *The Jungles of New Guinea*, a campaign that shed very little glory on General MacArthur. In a subsequent volume I shall deal with General MacArthur's little-known role in trying to restore Humpty Dumpty—in trying to give the British and the Dutch back their Asian colonies intact, and recreate the past. This was a definite part of his self-imposed role in 1945, when he went far beyond his directives from the Joint Chiefs of Staff and entered the political arena in Asia, the Philippines, and the Dutch East Indies particularly.

Outside this series I dealt with MacArthur's controversial management of the Korea war in my three-volume series *The Pusan Perimeter*, *On to the Yalu*, and *The Bloody Road to Panmunjom*.

In this volume of the Pacific war series General MacArthur is really shown at his best, showing personal bravery, a dedication to his self-imposed tasks, and a good deal of generosity and consideration for the men beneath him.

For much of the material relating to the naval battles of Surigao Strait, the Sulu Sea, Samar, and Cape Engano, I relied on research done earlier for my *The Battle of Leyte Gulf*, *The Kamikazes*, *The Men of the Gambier Bay*, and *McCampbell's Heroes*.

Barbey Daniel E. *MacArthur's Amphibious Navy*. Annapolis: Naval Institute Press, 1969.

Boei Sen Shi Shitsu. The 101-Volume Japanese official history of the Pacific war, published in the postwar years by the Japanese Self Defense Agency. For this book I used the volumes dealing with the New Guinea campaign, and the army and navy volumes on the Philippines campaign of defense in 1944 and 1945.

Breuer, William B. *Retaking the Philippines*. New York: St Martin's, 1986.

Eichelberger, Robert. *Our Jungle Road to Tokyo*. New York: Viking, 1950.

Evans, David C., ed. *The Japanese Navy in World War II*. Annapolis: Naval Institute Press, 1969.

Inoguchi, Rikihei, and Tadashi Nakajima, with Roger Pineau. *The Divine Wind*. Annapolis: Naval Institute Press, 1958.

James, Clayton. *The Years of MacArthur*, vol. II. Boston: Houghton-Mifflin, 1975.

Kenney, George C. *General Kenney Reports*. New York: Duell Sloan and Pearce, 1949.

Krueger, Walter. *From Down Under to Nippon, The Story of the Sixth Army in World War II*, Washington: Combat Forces Press, 1953.

Leary, William M., ed. *We Shall Return, MacArthur's Commanders and the Defeat of Japan*. Lexington, KY: University Press of Kentucky, 1988.

MacArthur, Douglas. *Reminiscences*. New York: McGraw-Hill, 1964.

Manchester, William L. *American Caesar*. Boston: Little Brown, 1978.

Morison, Samuel Eliot. *Leyte*. Boston: Atlantic, Little Brown, 1970.

Whitney, Courtney. *MacArthur, His Rendezvous with History*. New York: Knopf, 1956.

INDEX